Mediterranean Diet Cookbook for Beginners

2000 Days of Quick & Easy Mediterranean Diet Recipes for Beginners with a 60-Day Meal Plan & Weekly Shopping List | Full Color Pictures.

Embrace a Healthy Lifestyle without Sacrificing Flavor.

Emory Stout

TABLE OF CONTENTS

INTRODUCTION

Dear readers,

Welcome to "The Mediterranean Essence: A Path to Flavorful Well-being," your ultimate guide to a lifestyle enriched with zest and vigor. This expedition transcends the realm of mere dietary choices—it's a comprehensive approach to enhancing both your physical and spiritual well-being through the revered Mediterranean Diet.

Joining this journey means aligning with a community weary of the drabness of typical diet routines, baffled by conflicting health guidance, and eager to craft nourishing yet flavorful dishes. This book tackles these issues directly, offering a fusion of taste and health that's both enriching and satisfying.

Within these pages lies a collection of over 122 straightforward, inviting recipes that shed light on the Mediterranean Diet's core principles. Each dish is designed not only to please your palate but also to bolster your health and joy.

Guiding you through this culinary quest is Emory Stout, a seasoned chef and an ardent promoter of healthy living. With a rich background in culinary arts and nutrition, especially in dietary management of diabetes, Emory's recipes are time-honored, practical, and vibrant. His expertise in blending health with flavor is unmatched, making him the perfect mentor for your Mediterranean journey.

Embark on this life-altering path and discover a lifestyle that goes beyond mere dietary changes—a celebration of vitality, health, and the pleasure of every meal. Welcome to a new way of living, where every day is an opportunity to nourish yourself and delight in the bold, vibrant flavors of the Mediterranean.

Let's embark on this flavorful adventure together, turning each page toward a more fulfilled and healthier life.

CHAPTER 1: THE MEDITERRANEAN DIET: A JOURNEY TO HEALTH AND FLAVOR

The Basics of the Mediterranean Diet

Welcome to the enchanting world of the Mediterranean Diet, a culinary tradition celebrated not just for its delectable flavors but also for its remarkable health benefits. This chapter is your stepping stone into a lifestyle that harmonizes taste with well-being, offering you a comprehensive understanding of why the Mediterranean Diet stands out as a beacon of healthy living.

The Essence of the Mediterranean Diet

At its core, the Mediterranean Diet is more than just a list of foods to eat or avoid; it's a cultural heritage, rooted in the sun-drenched lands surrounding the Mediterranean Sea. The diet is a reflection of the lifestyle of people from this region, who have long enjoyed lower rates of chronic diseases and higher life expectancy compared to other parts of the world.

The Mediterranean Diet emphasizes:

Fruits and Vegetables – Pillars of Nutrition: Central to this diet are the varied and colorful fruits and vegetables, packed with vital nutrients, minerals, and fibers. They take center stage in meals, not just as accompaniments but as main attractions, enhancing the diet's fiber quotient, which supports digestion and aids in maintaining a healthy weight.

Fruits: Berries, apples, oranges, grapes, figs, melons, pears, and peaches.
Vegetables: Spinach, tomatoes, eggplants, bell peppers, onions, kale, carrots, and broccoli.

Vital Fats for Heart Health:

Olive Oil and More – The Diet's Liquid Gold: Olive oil, rich in monounsaturated fats and omega-3s, anchors this diet's fat intake, contributing to heart health by helping to lower cholesterol and reduce heart disease risk. The inclusion of avocados, nuts, and seeds adds a spectrum of beneficial fats.

Olive Oil: Use extra virgin olive oil in dressings and cooking.
Nuts and Seeds: Incorporate almonds, chia seeds, walnuts, and sunflower seeds into your diet.
Avocados: Rich in healthy fats, avocados are versatile and can be used in various recipes.

Proteins – Lean and Nutritious:

Seafood, Poultry, and Plant Proteins: The diet leans on fish, poultry, and legumes for protein, balancing nutrient intake while minimizing unhealthy fats, essential for maintaining health.

Fish Selection: trout, salmon, sardines, and mackerel.

Poultry Choices: skinless chicken or turkey, ideally grilled or baked.

Legumes Variety: Beans, chickpeas, and lentils are excellent choices.

Wholesome Grains – Essential and Nutritious:

Quinoa, Farro, and Whole Wheat: Say goodbye to refined grains and welcome the wholesome goodness of quinoa, farro, and whole wheat. These grains are fiber-rich powerhouses that serve as foundational elements in a myriad of dishes.

Breads and Pastas: Choose options crafted from whole wheat or other whole grains to elevate your meals with added nutrients and texture.

Ancient Grains: Embrace the nutritional heritage of grains like barley, quinoa, farro, and bulgur, each offering unique flavors and health benefits.

Rice: Switch to brown rice or wild rice selections, which provide more fiber and nutrients compared to white rice.

Dairy in Moderation:

Select Cheeses and Yogurts: The diet incorporates cheeses like feta, mozzarella and Greek yogurt, enjoyed in moderation, aiding in a balanced protein and calcium intake.

The Flavorful World of Herbs and Spices:

Natural Taste Enhancers: Utilizing herbs and spices not only boosts flavor but also offers health benefits, including anti-inflammatory effects, reducing the need for excess salt or fat, essential for reducing chronic disease risk.

Herbs: cilantro, basil, rosemary, thyme, and parsley in your dishes.

Spices: black pepper, nutmeg, cinnamon, and garlic.

The Wine Tradition:

Balanced Wine Enjoyment: True to the Mediterranean ethos, a moderate intake of wine, especially red, aligns with the diet's heart-friendly approach due to its antioxidants.

By integrating these elements, you're not just adopting a diet; you're embracing a lifestyle that celebrates rich flavors, diverse ingredients, and overall well-being.

Why Embrace the Mediterranean Diet?

Decades of research have illuminated the Mediterranean Diet's profound impact on health, showing consistent associations with reduced risks of heart disease, stroke, diabetes, and certain cancers. Its balance of macronutrients and focus on anti-inflammatory foods can aid in weight management, brain health, and longevity.

Embarking on Your Journey

Adopting the Mediterranean Diet is like embarking on a culinary voyage, where every meal is an opportunity to nourish your body and delight your senses. The following chapters will guide you through this journey, offering practical tips, easy-to-follow recipes, and insights into how to seamlessly integrate this diet into your lifestyle.

As you delve into the flavors and traditions of the Mediterranean, you'll discover that this diet is not about restriction or deprivation but about celebrating food, fostering community, and embracing a lifestyle that is as fulfilling as it is healthful.

Let's begin this journey together, exploring the rich tapestry of the Mediterranean Diet and how it can illuminate the path to health and vitality, one delicious meal at a time.

Mastering Mediterranean Techniques

Embracing the Mediterranean Diet isn't just about what you eat—it's also about how you prepare your meals. Mastering Mediterranean cooking techniques can transform simple ingredients into culinary masterpieces that nourish both body and soul. Let's delve into some key methods that define Mediterranean cuisine, ensuring that every dish you create is not only healthy but also brimming with flavor.

Grilling and Broiling: The Art of Fire

Grilling and broiling are quintessential Mediterranean techniques, perfect for enhancing the natural flavors of vegetables, fish, and lean meats without the need for excessive fats or oils. This method imparts a smoky essence and charred texture that can elevate a simple ingredient to something truly special. Whether you're grilling a whole fish, skewered vegetables, or chicken, the key is to allow the natural flavors to shine, complemented by herbs and a drizzle of olive oil.

Sautéing: Quick and Flavorful

Sautéing is a versatile technique in the Mediterranean kitchen, ideal for creating dishes that are vibrant and rich in flavor. Using a small amount of high-quality olive oil, you can quickly cook vegetables, garlic, and onions, creating a flavorful base for any dish. The secret is to keep the ingredients moving in the pan, allowing them to cook evenly while retaining their texture and nutritional value.

Slow Cooking: Unleashing Depth of Flavor

Slow cooking is a revered method in the Mediterranean tradition, perfect for stews, legumes, and braised dishes. This technique allows flavors to meld and deepen over time, creating dishes that are complex and comforting. By using a low and slow approach, you can transform simple ingredients into a meal that's both nutritious and satisfying, embodying the essence of Mediterranean hospitality.

Fresh Herbs: Aromatic Accents

In Mediterranean cooking, fresh herbs are not just garnishes; they're integral components that infuse dishes with freshness and aroma. Incorporating herbs like basil, oregano, rosemary, and thyme into your cooking not only adds layers of flavor but also boosts the health benefits of your meals, thanks to their antioxidant properties.

The Balance of Acidity and Fat

Understanding the balance between acidity and fat is crucial in Mediterranean cuisine. A squeeze of lemon juice, a splash of vinegar, or a touch of yogurt can elevate a dish, providing a counterpoint to the richness of olive oil and the savoriness of the ingredients. This interplay is key to achieving the vibrant, balanced flavors that define Mediterranean cooking.

By mastering these techniques, you're not just following recipes; you're adopting a culinary philosophy that celebrates the joy of cooking and the pleasure of eating healthfully. Each meal becomes an opportunity to explore the rich tapestry of Mediterranean flavors, creating dishes that are not only delicious but also deeply nourishing.

Essential Cooking Techniques for Beginners

Embarking on your culinary journey with the Mediterranean Diet doesn't require professional chef skills. Even as a beginner, you can create delicious, healthful meals by mastering a few basic cooking techniques. These methods are not only straightforward but also pivotal in preserving the nutritional integrity of your ingredients, allowing you to enjoy meals that are as nourishing as they are flavorful.

Roasting: Enhancing Flavors Naturally

Roasting is a technique that can bring out the natural sweetness and depth of flavor in vegetables and meats. By cooking ingredients slowly in an oven, you allow them to caramelize naturally, enhancing their taste and texture. This method is ideal for a beginner, as it requires minimal intervention—just a drizzle of olive oil, some herbs, and a pinch of salt are enough to transform simple ingredients into a delectable feast.

Poaching: Gentle Cooking for Delicate Ingredients

Poaching involves cooking ingredients, particularly fish or poultry, in a gentle simmering liquid. This method is excellent for preserving the delicate texture and flavor of the food, ensuring that it remains moist and tender. By infusing the poaching liquid with herbs, spices, or a splash of wine, you can impart subtle flavors to the ingredients, making each bite a delight.

Dressing and Marinades: Infusing Flavor Without the Fat

Creating your own dressings and marinades is a fundamental skill that can elevate even the simplest dishes. Using a base of olive oil and vinegar or lemon juice, you can experiment with different herbs and spices to create dressings that add a burst of flavor to salads or marinades that tenderize and enhance meats and vegetables.

Building Flavorful Bases: The Foundation of Great Dishes

Learning to build a flavorful base is crucial in Mediterranean cooking. Starting with ingredients like onions, garlic, and tomatoes, cooked slowly to develop their flavors, can serve as the foundation for countless dishes. This technique, known as sofrito in some Mediterranean regions, provides depth and richness to stews, sauces, and soups.

By mastering these essential cooking techniques, you're well on your way to creating Mediterranean dishes that are not only delicious and satisfying but also aligned with a healthy lifestyle. These methods empower you to cook with confidence, exploring the rich culinary heritage of the Mediterranean while nurturing your health and well-being.

Tips from a Professional Chef

Embarking on your Mediterranean culinary journey, it's invaluable to have insights from a professional chef who specializes in this healthful and flavorful cuisine. Here are some expert tips to help you navigate your kitchen like a pro, enhancing your cooking skills while adhering to the principles of the Mediterranean Diet.

Quality Over Quantity

Start with high-quality ingredients. The Mediterranean diet emphasizes freshness and quality, so choose local, seasonal produce, fresh fish, and high-quality olive oil. These ingredients not only taste better but also offer more nutritional benefits.

Simplicity is Key

Don't overcomplicate your dishes. Mediterranean cooking is about letting the natural flavors of the ingredients shine through. Use herbs and spices to enhance, not overpower, the main components of your dish.

Knife Skills Matter

Invest time in learning basic knife skills. Efficient and safe cutting techniques not only speed up your meal prep but also ensure your ingredients cook evenly, enhancing the dish's overall flavor and presentation.

The Art of Mise en Place

Practice mise en place, the culinary process of having all your ingredients prepped and ready to go before you start cooking. This organization helps streamline your cooking process, reduces stress, and ensures you don't forget any crucial components.

Balance Your Flavors

Understand the balance of flavors—sweet, salty, acidic, and bitter—and how they interact in a dish. Experiment with different combinations to find what works best for you, always aiming for a harmonious finish that excites the palate.

Master Heat Control

Get comfortable with controlling heat. Whether you're searing fish, simmering a stew, or roasting vegetables, knowing how to manage your heat source can make the difference between an okay dish and a fantastic one.

Don't Waste, Be Creative

Embrace the philosophy of zero waste. Use peels, bones, and leftovers to create stocks, sauces, or compost. This approach is not only eco-friendly but also a testament to the resourcefulness inherent in Mediterranean cooking.

Taste As You Go

Remember to taste your food as you cook. Adjusting seasonings throughout the cooking process is key to developing a well-rounded flavor profile.

Invest in High-Quality Cookware

Quality cookware can significantly impact your cooking efficiency and the final outcome of your dishes. Invest in a good set of knives, a durable set of pots and pans, and specialized tools like a mortar and pestle or a tagine to authentically prepare Mediterranean dishes.

Presentation Matters

Finally, take time to present your dishes beautifully. Eating is a sensory experience that involves sight as well as taste and smell. A well-presented dish enhances the dining experience, making the meal more enjoyable and satisfying.

By incorporating these tips into your cooking routine, you'll deepen your understanding of Mediterranean cuisine and develop skills that will serve you well in any culinary endeavor. Here's to a journey filled with delicious discoveries and healthful eating!

CHAPTER 2: 60-DAY MEAL PLAN

Day	Breakfast (400 kcal)	Lunch (500 kcal)	Snack (220 kcal)	Dinner (380 kcal)
Day 1	Mediterranean Feta and Olive Omelette - p.23	Provencal Vegetable Soup with Pesto - p.43	Olive Tapenade on Whole Grain Crackers - p.64	Baked Trout with Almond and Parsley Crust - p.81
Day 2	Herbed Chicken and Vegetable Skillet - p.23	Asparagus and Lemon Zest Risotto - p.54	Mini Berry and Mascarpone Tarts - p.73	Spinach and Feta Stuffed Portobello Mushrooms - p.83
Day 3	Grilled Tomato and Mozzarella Caprese Salad - p.24	Andalusian Gazpacho with Almonds - p.44	Avocado and Lime Guacamole with Baked Pita Chips - p.65	Grilled Tuna Steak with Tomato Olive Salsa - p.82
Day 4	Sundried Tomato and Spinach Quiche Cups - p.24	Lasagna with Vegetables and Ricotta - p.52	Rosemary and Grape Focaccia Bites - p.65	Grilled Zucchini and Bell Pepper with Feta - p.85
Day 5	Eggplant and Zucchini Frittata - p.25	Hearty Provencal Lamb Stew with Herbes de Provence - p.46	Oat and Nut Protein Bars - p.67	Grilled Sardines with Olive Tapenade - p.84
Day 6	Ricotta and Spinach Bake - p.25	Pasta Puttanesca - p.48	Fig and Honey Cheesecake - p.76	Cauliflower Steaks with Tahini Drizzle - p.85
Day 7	Garlic Mushroom and Herb Polenta - p.26	Farfalle with Spinach Pesto and Pine Nuts - p.49	Raspberry Ricotta Mini Galettes - p.68	Pan-Seared Tilapia with Lemon Caper Sauce - p.84
Day 8	Cucumber Feta Yogurt Bowl - p.26	Moussaka - p.62	Mixed Berry and Yogurt Parfait - p.68	Stewed Artichokes with Lemon - p.86
Day 9	Cherry Tomato and Basil Scramble - p.27	Lentil Soup with Vegetables and Thyme - p.43	Date and Almond Energy Balls - p.69	Provencal Nicoise Salad - p.88
Day 10	Artichoke and Parmesan Breakfast Bake - p.27	Tortellini with Spinach and Walnut Pesto - p.50	Cherry and Almond Clafoutis - p.75	Mediterranean Chickpea Salad with Herbs and Feta - p.89
Day 11	Lemon Ricotta Pancakes - p.28	Tomato Basil Risotto with Mozzarella - p.54	Almond and Orange Blossom Biscotti - p.71	Falafel with Tahina and Fresh Vegetables - p.86

Day	Breakfast (400 kcal)	Lunch (500 kcal)	Snack (220 kcal)	Dinner (380 kcal)
Day 12	Spinach and Feta Stuffed Crepes - p.28	Pesto Penne with Roasted Cherry Tomatoes and Almonds - p.51	Mini Lemon and Olive Oil Cakes - p.71	Herb-Grilled Salmon with Lemon Quinoa - p.93
Day 13	Halloumi and Avocado Breakfast Salad - p.29	Seafood Paella - p.56	Ricotta and Fig Crostini with Honey Drizzle - p.72	Tabbouleh with Couscous and Numerous Herbs - p.89
Day 14	Turkey and Spinach Breakfast Meatballs - p.29	Pizza Margherita - p.52	Sesame and Honey Halva Squares - p.72	Shrimp and Feta Baked in Tomato Sauce, Served with Spinach - p.94
Day 15	Peachy Cottage Cheese Delight - p.31	Italian Pork Ragu with Porcini Mushrooms - p.46	Peanut Butter and Jelly Energy Bites - p.67	Fig, Prosciutto, and Arugula Salad - p.90
Day 16	Smoked Salmon and Cream Cheese Bagel - p.31	Provencal Vegetable Soup with Pesto - p.43	Espresso Affogato with Vanilla Gelato - p.73	Baked Trout with Almond and Parsley Crust - p.81
Day 17	Avocado Toast With Poached Egg and Feta - p.32	Moroccan Lamb Tagine - p.45	Apricot and Walnut Phyllo Cups - p.74	Broccoli and Quinoa Salad with Honey Mustard Dressing - p.81
Day 18	Grilled Portobello Mushrooms with Eggs - p.32	Risotto with Grilled Eggplant and Balsamic - p.55	Pomegranate and Yogurt Mousse - p.74	Cajun-Spiced Shrimp and Cauliflower Grits - p.82
Day 19	Tuna and White Bean Breakfast Salad - p.33	Spaghetti Carbonara - p.48	Lemon Sorbet with Mint - p.75	Cajun-Spiced Shrimp and Cauliflower Grits - p.82
Day 20	Chicken Sausage and Vegetable Skillet - p.33	Gyros - p.59	Cherry and Almond Clafoutis - p.75	Quinoa Salad with Roasted Vegetables - p.91
Day 21	Greek Yogurt and Mixed Berry Parfait - p.34	Pasta Puttanesca - p.48	Figs Stuffed with Mascarpone and Honey - p.76	Pan-Seared Tilapia with Lemon Caper Sauce - p.84
Day 22	Beef and Spinach Breakfast Hash - p.34	Chicken Parmesan (Parmigiana) - p.62	Fig and Honey Cheesecake - p.76	Spinach and Feta Stuffed Portobello Mushrooms - p.83

Day	Breakfast (400 kcal)	Lunch (500 kcal)	Snack (220 kcal)	Dinner (380 kcal)
Day 23	Egg and Turkey Bacon Muffins - p.35	Pasta with Chicken, Artichokes, and Cream Sauce - p.51	Raspberry and Dark Chocolate Macaroons - p.77	Grilled Sardines with Olive Tapenade - p.84
Day 24	Protein-Packed Breakfast Tacos - p.35	Penne Arrabbiata with Olives - p.49	Almond and Raspberry Clafoutis - p.77	Grilled Zucchini and Bell Pepper with Feta - p.85
Day 25	Berry Barley Breakfast Bowl - p.40	Risotto with Porcini Mushrooms and Thyme - p.61	Apricot and Pistachio Tartlets - p.78	Baked Haddock with a Mediterranean Salsa Verde - p.96
Day 26	Banana Almond Oatmeal - p.40	Hearty Provencal Lamb Stew with Herbes de Provence - p.46	Lemon Lavender Shortbread - p.78	Falafel with Tahina and Fresh Vegetables - p.86
Day 27	Spiced Pumpkin Quinoa Breakfast Bowl - p.41	Tortellini with Spinach and Walnut Pesto - p.50	Orange and Almond Flourless Cake - p.79	Mussels in Garlic White Wine Sauce with a Side of Grilled Asparagus - p.95
Day 28	Apricot and Hazelnut Bulgur - p.41	Moussaka - p.62	Berry and Mascarpone Tart - p.79	Provencal Nicoise Salad - p.88
Day 29	Crete Avocado and Pineapple Creaminess - p.37	Pork Souvlaki with Tzatziki - p.58	Mini Bell Peppers Stuffed with Feta and Dill - p.64	Tabbouleh with Couscous and Numerous Herbs - p.88
Day 30	Rhodes Raspberry and Oat Fuel - p.37	Andalusian Gazpacho with Almonds - p.44	Rosemary and Grape Focaccia Bites - p.65	Shrimp and Avocado Salad with Citrus Vinaigrette - p.90
Day 31	Garlic Mushroom and Herb Polenta - p.26	Turkey and Spinach Meatballs in Lemon Broth - p.61	Olive Tapenade on Whole Grain Crackers - p.64	Grilled Eggplant and Tomato Salad with Basil - p.91
Day 32	Eggplant and Zucchini Frittata - p.25	Lentil Soup with Vegetables and Thyme - p.43	Oat and Nut Protein Bars - p.67	Pan-Seared Tilapia with Lemon Caper Sauce - p.84
Day 33	Peachy Cottage Cheese Delight - p.31	Orzo with Grilled Vegetables and Feta Cheese - p.50	Avocado and Lime Guacamole with Baked Pita Chips - p.65	Cauliflower Steaks with Tahini Drizzle - p.85

Day	Breakfast (400 kcal)	Lunch (500 kcal)	Snack (220 kcal)	Dinner (380 kcal)
Day 34	Protein-Packed Breakfast Tacos - p.35	Provencal Vegetable Soup with Pesto - p.43	Espresso Affogato with Vanilla Gelato - p.73	Crab Cakes with Remoulade and a Light Coleslaw - p.96
Day 35	Halloumi and Avocado Breakfast Salad - p.29	Braised Beef with Mediterranean Herbs and Tomatoes - p.61	Date and Almond Energy Balls - p.69	Stewed Artichokes with Lemon - p.86
Day 36	Herbed Chicken and Vegetable Skillet - p.23	Pesto Penne with Roasted Cherry Tomatoes and Almonds - p.51	Peanut Butter and Jelly Energy Bites - p.67	Cajun-Spiced Shrimp and Cauliflower Grits - p.82
Day 37	Ricotta and Spinach Bake - p.25	Turkish Beef and Eggplant Stew - p.45	Mixed Berry and Yogurt Parfait - p.68	Zucchini Noodles with Pesto and Cherry Tomatoes - p.83
Day 38	Lemon Ricotta Pancakes - p.28	Pizza Margherita - p.52	Oat and Nut Protein Bars - p.67	Provencal Nicoise Salad - p.88
Day 39	Smoked Salmon and Cream Cheese Bagel - p.31	Spaghetti Carbonara - p.48	Mini Berry and Mascarpone Tarts - p.73	Broccoli and Quinoa Salad with Honey Mustard Dressing - p.81
Day 40	Cucumber Feta Yogurt Bowl - p.26	Hearty Provencal Lamb Stew with Herbes de Provence - p.46	Espresso Affogato with Vanilla Gelato - p.73	Falafel with Tahina and Fresh Vegetables - p.86
Day 41	Cherry Tomato and Basil Scramble - p.27	Greek Lemon Chicken Orzo Soup - p.44	Apricot and Walnut Phyllo Cups - p.74	Baked Trout with Almond and Parsley Crust, Served with Arugula Salad - p.821
Day 42	Artichoke and Parmesan Breakfast Bake - p.27	Italian Pork Ragu with Porcini Mushrooms - p.46	Lemon Sorbet with Mint - p.75	Spinach and Feta Stuffed Portobello Mushrooms - p.83
Day 43	Grilled Tomato and Mozzarella Caprese Salad - p.24	Pumpkin and Gorgonzola Risotto - p.55	Raspberry Ricotta Mini Galettes - p.68	Herb-Grilled Salmon with Lemon Quinoa - p.93
Day 44	Sundried Tomato and Spinach Quiche Cups - p.24	Pasta Puttanesca - p.48	Mixed Berry and Yogurt Parfait - p.68	Quinoa Salad with Roasted Vegetables - p.91

Day	Breakfast (400 kcal)	Lunch (500 kcal)	Snack (220 kcal)	Dinner (380 kcal)
Day 45	Eggplant and Zucchini Frittata - p.25	Farfalle with Spinach Pesto and Pine Nuts - p.49	Peanut Butter and Jelly Energy Bites - p.67	Grilled Sardines with Olive Tapenade - p.84
Day 46	Ricotta and Spinach Bake - p.25	Chicken Cacciatore with Olives and Capers - p.59	Olive Tapenade on Whole Grain Crackers - p.64	Grilled Eggplant and Tomato Salad with Basil - p.91
Day 47	Lemon Ricotta Pancakes - p.28	Lasagna with Vegetables and Ricotta - p.52	Raspberry and Dark Chocolate Macaroons - p.77	Falafel with Tahina and Fresh Vegetables - p.86
Day 48	Spinach and Feta Stuffed Crepes - p.28	Orzo with Grilled Vegetables and Feta Cheese - p.50	Avocado and Lime Guacamole with Baked Pita Chips - p.65	Salad with Smoked Salmon, Avocado, and Green Salad - p.89
Day 49	Halloumi and Avocado Breakfast Salad - p.29	Grilled Skirt Steak with Chimichurri Sauce - p.60	Rosemary and Grape Focaccia Bites - p.65	Fig, Prosciutto, and Arugula Salad - p.90
Day 50	Turkey and Spinach Breakfast Meatballs - p.29	Asparagus and Lemon Zest Risotto - p.54	Date and Almond Energy Balls - p.69	Squid Stuffed with Herbed Couscous and Tomato Sauce - p.95
Day 51	Peachy Cottage Cheese Delight - p.31	Gyros - p.59	Pomegranate and Yogurt Mousse - p.74	Tabbouleh with Couscous and Numerous Herbs - p.88
Day 52	Smoked Salmon and Cream Cheese Bagel - p.31	Pizza Margherita - p.52	Mini Lemon and Olive Oil Cakes - p.71	Mussels in Garlic White Wine Sauce with a Side of Grilled Asparagus - p.95
Day 53	Avocado Toast With Poached Egg and Feta - p.32	Pork Tenderloin with Fig and Balsamic Reduction - p.60	Mixed Berry and Yogurt Parfait - p.68	Mediterranean Chickpea Salad with Herbs and Feta - p.89
Day 54	Grilled Portobello Mushrooms with Eggs - p.32	Tortellini with Spinach and Walnut Pesto - p.50	Raspberry Ricotta Mini Galettes - p.68	Herb-Grilled Salmon with Lemon Quinoa - p.93
Day 55	Tuna and White Bean Breakfast Salad - p.33	Braised Beef with Mediterranean Herbs and Tomatoes - p.61	Lemon Lavender Shortbread - p.78	Broccoli and Quinoa Salad with Honey Mustard Dressing - p.81

Day	Breakfast (400 kcal)	Lunch (500 kcal)	Snack (220 kcal)	Dinner (380 kcal)
Day 56	Chicken Sausage and Vegetable Skillet - p.33	Pesto Penne with Roasted Cherry Tomatoes and Almonds - p.51	Fig and Honey Cheesecake - p.76	Grilled Tuna Steak with Tomato Olive Salsa - p.82
Day 57	Crete Avocado and Pineapple Creaminess - p.37	Seafood Paella - p.56	Almond and Orange Blossom Biscotti - p.71	Spinach and Feta Stuffed Portobello Mushrooms - p.83
Day 58	Rhodes Raspberry and Oat Fuel - p.37	Greek Lemon Chicken Orzo Soup - p.44	Mini Berry and Mascarpone Tarts - p.73	Grilled Sardines with Olive Tapenade - p.84
Day 59	Sicilian Almond and Banana Powerhouse - p.38	Pasta Puttanesca - p.48	Espresso Affogato with Vanilla Gelato - p.73	Cauliflower Steaks with Tahini Drizzle - p.85
Day 60	Ionian Island Kiwi and Spinach Zest - p.38	Italian Pork Ragu with Porcini Mushrooms - p.46	Sesame and Honey Halva Squares - p.72	Falafel with Tahina and Fresh Vegetables - p.86

Note: The 60-Day Meal Plan featured in this book serves as a guiding framework and a source of culinary inspiration. The calorie estimates provided for each dish are approximate and can vary based on portion sizes and the specific ingredients used. Our meal plan is crafted to offer a varied and balanced array of options, abundant in proteins, healthy fats, and carbohydrates, enabling you to pursue a nutritious diet while still relishing the pleasure of daily gourmet meals.

Should you notice that the caloric values of the recipes don't precisely match your unique dietary requirements or preferences, don't hesitate to adjust the serving sizes. Modify them upwards or downwards to tailor the meal plan to your individual health objectives and taste preferences. Embrace your creativity and savor each meal in a way that best suits your dietary journey!

CHAPTER 3: BREAKFASTS
Classic Breakfasts Reimagined: A Mediterranean Touch

Mediterranean Feta and Olive Omelette

Prep: 5 minutes | Cook: 10 minutes | Serves: 2

Ingredients:

- 4 large eggs (220g)
- 1/4 cup crumbled feta cheese (50g)
- 1/4 cup chopped olives (30g)
- 1 tbsp chopped fresh parsley (3.8g)
- 1 tbsp olive oil (15ml)
- Salt and pepper to taste

Instructions:

1. Beat the eggs in a bowl and mix in the feta cheese, olives, and parsley. Season with salt and pepper.
2. Heat the olive oil in a skillet over medium heat. Pour in the egg mixture.
3. Cook until the eggs are set but slightly runny in the center, about 4-5 minutes. Fold the omelette in half and cook for another 2 minutes.
4. Serve the omelette hot.

Nutritional Facts (Per Serving): Calories: 400 | Sugars: 2g | Fat: 31g | Carbohydrates: 3g | Protein: 22g | Fiber: 0g | Sodium: 700g

Herbed Chicken and Vegetable Breakfast Skillet

Prep: 10 minutes | Cook: 20 minutes | Serves: 2

Ingredients:

- 2 chicken breasts diced (6 oz each, 170g each)
- 1 cup chopped bell peppers (150g)
- 1 cup chopped zucchini (150g)
- 1/2 cup chopped onions (75g)
- 2 cloves garlic, minced
- 1 tbsp olive oil (15 ml)
- 1 tsp mixed herbs (thyme, rosemary) (5 ml)
- Salt and pepper to taste

Instructions:

1. Heat olive oil in a skillet over medium heat. Add garlic and onions, sauté until translucent.
2. Add chicken breasts, seasoned with salt, pepper, and mixed herbs. Cook until browned on both sides.
3. Add bell peppers and zucchini, cook until vegetables are tender and chicken is cooked through.
4. Serve hot directly from the skillet.

Nutritional Facts (Per Serving): Calories: 400 | Sugars: 6g | Fat: 20g | Carbohydrates: 20g | Protein: 40g | Fiber: 3g | Sodium: 70mg

Grilled Tomato and Mozzarella Caprese Salad

Prep: 10 minutes | Cook: 5 minutes | Serves: 2

Ingredients:

- 2 large tomatoes, sliced (400g)
- 8 oz mozzarella cheese, sliced (225g)
- 1/4 cup fresh basil leaves (15g)
- 2 tbsp olive oil (30 ml)
- 1 tbsp balsamic vinegar (15 ml)
- Salt and pepper to taste

Instructions:

1. Grill tomato slices over medium heat for 2 minutes per side.
2. Arrange tomato and mozzarella slices alternately on a plate, sprinkle with basil leaves.
3. Drizzle with olive oil and balsamic vinegar. Season with salt and pepper.

Nutritional Facts (Per Serving): Calories: 400 | Sugars: 6g | Fat: 30g | Carbohydrates: 10g | Protein: 22g | Fiber: 2g | Sodium: 300mg

Sundried Tomato and Spinach Quiche Cups

Prep: 10 minutes | Cook: 25 minutes | Serves: 4

Ingredients:

- 4 large eggs (220g)
- 1/4 cup milk (60ml)
- 1/2 cup chopped spinach (15g)
- 1/4 cup chopped sundries tomatoes (28g)
- 1/4 cup shredded mozzarella cheese (28g)
- 1 tbsp olive oil (15ml)
- Salt and pepper to taste

Instructions:

1. Preheat the oven to 375°F (190°C). Grease a muffin tin with olive oil.
2. In a bowl, whisk together the eggs, milk, salt, and pepper.
3. Stir in the spinach, sundries tomatoes, and mozzarella cheese.
4. Pour the mixture into the muffin tin, filling each cup about 3/4 full.
5. Bake for 20-25 minutes, or until the quiche cups are set and lightly golden on top.
6. Let cool for 5 minutes before serving.

Nutritional Facts (Per Serving): Calories: 400 | Sugars: 4g | Fat: 28g | Carbohydrates: 12g | Protein: 24g | Fiber: 2g | Sodium: 400g

Eggplant and Zucchini Frittata

Prep: 10 minutes | Cook: 20 minutes | Serves: 4

Ingredients:

- 6 large eggs (330g)
- 1 cup diced eggplant (134g)
- 1 cup diced zucchini (124g)
- 1/4 cup milk (60ml)
- 1/2 cup shredded Parmesan cheese (50g)
- 2 Tbsp olive oil (30ml)
- 1 tsp salt (5g)
- 1/2 tsp black pepper (1g)
- 1 Tbsp chopped fresh basil (3.8g)

Instructions:

1. Preheat the oven to 375°F (190°C).
2. Heat olive oil in a skillet over medium heat. Add eggplant and zucchini, sautéing until softened, about 5 minutes.
3. In a bowl, whisk together eggs, milk, salt, and pepper. Stir in the sautéed vegetables and Parmesan cheese.
4. Pour the mixture into a greased 9-inch pie dish or oven-safe skillet.
5. Bake in the preheated oven until the frittata is set and lightly golden, about 15 minutes.
6. Garnish with chopped basil before serving.

Nutritional Facts (Per Serving): Calories: 400 | Sugars: 5g | Fat: 28g | Carbohydrates: 10g | Protein: 24g | Fiber: 2g | Sodium: 800g

Ricotta and Spinach Bake

Prep: 15 minutes | Cook: 30 minutes | Serves: 4

Ingredients:

- 1 cup ricotta cheese (250g)
- 2 cups fresh spinach, chopped (60g)
- 1 large egg
- 1/4 cup grated Parmesan cheese (25g)
- 1/2 tsp nutmeg (2.5 ml)
- Salt and pepper to taste

Instructions:

1. Preheat oven to 375°F (190°C). In a bowl, mix ricotta, spinach, egg, Parmesan, nutmeg, salt, and pepper.
2. Pour the mixture into a greased baking dish. Bake for 30 minutes or until set and lightly golden on top.
3. Let it cool slightly before serving.

Nutritional Facts (Per Serving): Calories: 400 | Sugars: 2g | Fat: 30g | Carbohydrates: 10g | Protein: 25g | Fiber: 1g | Sodium: 200mg

Garlic Mushroom and Herb Polenta

Prep: 5 minutes | Cook: 25 minutes | Serves: 4

Ingredients:

- 1 cup polenta (cornmeal) (160g)
- 4 cups water (960ml)
- 1 tsp salt (5g)
- 2 Tbsp olive oil (30ml)
- 1 cup sliced mushrooms (70g)
- 2 garlic cloves, minced (6g)
- 1/4 cup grated Parmesan cheese (25g)
- 1 Tbsp chopped fresh thyme (3.8g)
- 1 Tbsp chopped fresh parsley (3.8g)

Instructions:

1. Bring water to a boil in a saucepan. Add salt and slowly whisk in the polenta.
2. Reduce heat to low and cook, stirring frequently, until polenta is thick and creamy, about 20 minutes.
3. Meanwhile, heat olive oil in a skillet over medium heat. Add garlic and mushrooms, sautéing until tender, about 5 minutes.
4. Stir the cooked mushrooms, Parmesan cheese, thyme, and parsley into the polenta.
5. Serve the polenta warm.

Nutritional Facts (Per Serving): Calories: 400 | Sugars: 2g | Fat: 14g | Carbohydrates: 54g | Protein: 12g | Fiber: 4g | Sodium: 600g

Cucumber Feta Yogurt Bowl

Prep: 5 minutes | Cook: 0 minutes | Serves: 2

Ingredients:

- 1 cup Greek yogurt (245g)
- 1/2 cup diced cucumber (75g)
- 1/4 cup crumbled feta cheese (50g)
- 1 Tbsp olive oil (15ml)
- 1 Tbsp lemon juice (15ml)
- 1 tsp fresh dill, chopped (0.5g)
- Salt and pepper to taste

Instructions:

1. In a bowl, combine Greek yogurt, diced cucumber, crumbled feta cheese, olive oil, lemon juice, and chopped dill.
2. Season with salt and pepper to taste.
3. Divide the mixture into two bowls and serve chilled.

Nutritional Facts (Per Serving): Calories: 400 | Sugars: 8g | Fat: 32g | Carbohydrates: 12g | Protein: 18g | Fiber: 0g | Sodium: 500g

Cherry Tomato and Basil Scramble

Prep: 5 minutes | Cook: 10 minutes | Serves: 2

Ingredients:

- 4 large eggs (220g)
- 1/2 cup cherry tomatoes, halved (75g)
- 1/4 cup fresh basil, chopped (6g)
- 2 Tbsp milk (30ml)
- 1 Tbsp olive oil (15ml)
- Salt and pepper to taste

Instructions:

1. In a bowl, whisk together eggs, milk, salt, and pepper.
2. Heat olive oil in a skillet over medium heat. Add the egg mixture and cherry tomatoes.
3. Cook, stirring gently, until the eggs are set but still moist.
4. Remove from heat and stir in fresh basil.
5. Serve immediately.

Nutritional Facts (Per Serving): Calories: 400 | Sugars: 3g | Fat: 30g | Carbohydrates: 4g | Protein: 24g | Fiber: 1g | Sodium: 400g

Artichoke and Parmesan Breakfast Bake

Prep: 15 minutes | Cook: 25 minutes | Serves: 4

Ingredients:

- 6 large eggs (330g)
- 1 cup canned artichoke hearts, drained and chopped (200g)
- 1/2 cup grated Parmesan cheese (50g)
- 1/2 cup milk (120ml)
- 1/4 cup chopped fresh parsley (15g)
- 2 Tbsp olive oil (30ml)
- Salt and pepper to taste

Instructions:

1. Preheat the oven to 375°F (190°C). Grease a baking dish with olive oil.
2. In a large bowl, whisk together eggs, milk, salt, and pepper.
3. Stir in artichoke hearts, Parmesan cheese, and chopped parsley.
4. Pour the mixture into the prepared baking dish.
5. Bake in the preheated oven until the eggs are set and the top is lightly golden, about 25 minutes.
6. Let cool for a few minutes before serving.

Nutritional Facts (Per Serving): Calories: 400 | Sugars: 3g | Fat: 28g | Carbohydrates: 10g | Protein: 24g | Fiber: 2g | Sodium: 700g

Lemon Ricotta Pancakes

Prep: 10 minutes | Cook: 15 minutes | Serves: 4

Ingredients:

- 1 cup all-purpose flour (125g)
- 2 Tbsp sugar (25g)
- 1 tsp baking powder (5g)
- 1/2 tsp baking soda (2.5g)
- 1/4 tsp salt (1.25g)
- 3/4 cup ricotta cheese (180g)
- 1/2 cup milk (120ml)
- 2 large eggs (100g)
- Zest of 1 lemon
- 2 Tbsp lemon juice (30ml)
- 1 Tbsp melted unsalted butter (14g), plus extra for cooking

Instructions:

1. In a large bowl, whisk together flour, sugar, baking powder, baking soda, and salt.
2. In another bowl, mix ricotta cheese, milk, eggs, lemon zest, lemon juice, and melted butter until smooth.
3. Combine the wet ingredients with the dry ingredients, stirring until just mixed.
4. Heat a non-stick pan over medium heat and brush with a little butter. Pour 1/4 cup (60ml) of batter for each pancake and cook until bubbles form on the surface, then flip and cook until golden brown.
5. Serve warm with a drizzle of honey or maple syrup.

Nutritional Facts (Per Serving): Calories: 400 | Sugars: 12g | Fat: 18g | Carbohydrates: 42g | Protein: 16g | Fiber: 1g | Sodium: 400g

Spinach and Feta Stuffed Crepes

Prep: 20 minutes | Cook: 10 minutes | Serves: 4

Ingredients:

For the crepes:
- 1 cup all-purpose flour (125g)
- 1 1/2 cups milk (360ml)
- 2 large eggs (100g)
- 2 Tbsp melted unsalted butter (28g), plus extra for cooking
- 1/4 tsp salt (1.25g)

For the filling:
- 1 cup spinach, chopped (30g)
- 1/2 cup feta cheese, crumbled (75g)
- 1/4 cup ricotta cheese (60g)
- Salt and pepper to taste

Instructions:

1. For the crepes, blend flour, milk, eggs, melted butter, and salt until smooth. Let the batter rest for 10 minutes.
2. Heat a non-stick skillet over medium heat, brush with butter. Pour 1/4 cup (60ml) of batter, swirling to coat the bottom. Cook until the edge peels off easily, flip and cook for another 30 seconds. Repeat with remaining batter.
3. For the filling, mix spinach, feta, and ricotta cheese in a bowl. Season with salt and pepper.
4. Fill each crepe with the spinach and cheese mixture, fold and serve warm.

Nutritional Facts (Per Serving): Calories: 400 | Sugars: 6g | Fat: 22g | Carbohydrates: 34g | Protein: 18g | Fiber: 1g | Sodium: 700g

Halloumi and Avocado Breakfast Salad

Prep: 10 minutes | Cook: 5 minutes | Serves: 2

Ingredients:

- 1 cup mixed salad greens (30g)
- 4 oz halloumi cheese, sliced (113g)
- 1 avocado, sliced (200g)
- 2 Tbsp olive oil (30ml), divided
- 1 Tbsp lemon juice (15ml)
- Salt and pepper to taste
- 1/2 cup cherry tomatoes, halved (75g)

Instructions:

1. Heat 1 tablespoon of olive oil in a pan over medium heat. Add halloumi slices and cook until golden brown on both sides, about 2 minutes per side.
2. In a large bowl, toss the salad greens, cherry tomatoes, and avocado slices with the remaining olive oil and lemon juice. Season with salt and pepper.
3. Top the salad with the grilled halloumi and serve immediately.

Nutritional Facts (Per Serving): Calories: 400 | Sugars: 3g | Fat: 34g | Carbohydrates: 15g | Protein: 16g | Fiber: 7g | Sodium: 600g

Turkey and Spinach Breakfast Meatballs with Spiced Tomato Sauce

Prep: 15 minutes | Cook: 25 minutes | Serves: 4

Ingredients:

- 1 lb ground turkey (450g)
- 1 cup fresh spinach, chopped (30g)
- 1 tsp cumin (5 ml)
- 1/2 tsp smoked paprika (2.5 ml)
- 1 cup tomato sauce (250 ml)
- 1/2 tsp chili flakes (2.5 ml)
- Salt and pepper to taste

Instructions:

1. Mix ground turkey with spinach, cumin, smoked paprika, salt, and pepper. Form into small meatballs.
2. Cook meatballs in a skillet over medium heat until browned and cooked through, about 15 minutes.
3. In a separate saucepan, heat tomato sauce with chili flakes, simmer for 10 minutes.
4. Serve meatballs topped with spiced tomato sauce.

Nutritional Facts (Per Serving): Calories: 400 | Sugars: 5g | Fat: 20g | Carbohydrates: 15g | Protein: 35g | Fiber: 3g | Sodium: 300mg

CHAPTER 4: BREAKFASTS
High-Protein Mornings: Quick and Nutritious Solutions

Peachy Cottage Cheese Delight

Prep: 5 minutes | Cook: 0 minutes | Serves: 2

Ingredients:

- 1 cup cottage cheese (226g)
- 1 large peach, sliced (150g)
- 2 Tbsp honey (40ml)
- 1/4 cup granola (30g)
- 1 Tbsp sliced almonds (6g)
- 1/2 tsp cinnamon (1.3g)

Instructions:

1. Divide the cottage cheese between two bowls.
2. Top with sliced peach, drizzle with honey, and sprinkle with granola, sliced almonds, and cinnamon.
3. Serve immediately for a refreshing and nutritious breakfast or snack.

Nutritional Facts (Per Serving): Calories: 400 | Sugars: 31g | Fat: 10g | Carbohydrates: 58g | Protein: 20g | Fiber: 3g | Sodium: 500g

Smoked Salmon and Cream Cheese Bagel

Prep: 5 minutes | Cook: 0 minutes | Serves: 2

Ingredients:

- 2 whole wheat bagels (170g each)
- 4 oz smoked salmon (113g)
- 2 Tbsp cream cheese (30g)
- 2 slices red onion, thin (25g)
- 4 slices cucumber (28g)
- 1 Tbsp capers (8.6g)
- 1/4 tsp black pepper (0.5g)

Instructions:

1. Slice the bagels in half and toast until golden brown.
2. Spread cream cheese evenly over the cut sides of the bagel halves.
3. Layer smoked salmon, red onion, cucumber slices, and capers on top of each bagel half.
4. Sprinkle with black pepper and serve immediately.

Nutritional Facts (Per Serving): Calories: 400 | Sugars: 8g | Fat: 12g | Carbohydrates: 50g | Protein: 24g | Fiber: 6g | Sodium: 950g

Avocado Toast With Poached Egg and Feta Cheese

Prep: 10 minutes | Cook: 5 minutes | Serves: 1

Ingredients:

- 1 slice whole grain bread (50g)
- 1/2 avocado, mashed (100g)
- 1 egg
- 1 oz feta cheese, crumbled (28g)
- Salt and pepper to taste
- 1/2 tsp red pepper flakes (2.5 ml)

Instructions:

1. Toast the bread until golden and crispy.
2. Spread the mashed avocado on the toast.
3. Poach the egg in simmering water for about 4 minutes or until the whites are set but the yolk is still runny.
4. Place the poached egg on the avocado toast, sprinkle with feta cheese, red pepper flakes, salt, and pepper.

Nutritional Facts (Per Serving): Calories: 400 | Sugars: 3g | Fat: 25g | Carbohydrates: 30g | Protein: 20g | Fiber: 7g | Sodium: 400mg

Grilled Portobello Mushrooms with Poached Eggs

Prep: 10 minutes | Cook: 15 minutes | Serves: 2

Ingredients:

- 2 large portobello mushrooms, stems removed (100g each)
- 2 tbsp olive oil (30 ml)
- 2 eggs
- Salt and pepper to taste
- 1 tbsp chopped parsley (15 ml)
- 1/4 tsp garlic powder (1.25 ml)

Instructions:

1. Brush the portobello mushrooms with olive oil and season with salt, pepper, and garlic powder.
2. Grill the mushrooms over medium heat for about 5-7 minutes per side.
3. While the mushrooms are grilling, poach the eggs in simmering water for about 4 minutes.
4. Place a poached egg on each mushroom cap, sprinkle with parsley, salt, and pepper.

Nutritional Facts (Per Serving): Calories: 400 | Sugars: 2g | Fat: 30g | Carbohydrates: 10g | Protein: 18g | Fiber: 2g | Sodium: 200mg

Tuna and White Bean Breakfast Salad

Prep: 10 minutes | Cook: 0 minutes | Serves: 2

Ingredients:

- 1 can tuna in water, drained (140g)
- 1 cup canned white beans, rinsed and drained (170g)
- 2 cups mixed salad greens (60g)
- 2 Tbsp olive oil (30ml)
- 1 Tbsp lemon juice (15ml)
- Salt and pepper to taste
- 1/4 tsp dried oregano (0.5g)
- 1/4 cup chopped red onion (40g)

Instructions:

1. In a large bowl, combine the tuna, white beans, salad greens, and red onion.
2. In a small bowl, whisk together olive oil, lemon juice, salt, pepper, and oregano to make the dressing.
3. Pour the dressing over the salad and toss gently to combine.
4. Serve the salad immediately, or chill in the refrigerator before serving.

Nutritional Facts (Per Serving): Calories: 400 | Sugars: 2g | Fat: 20g | Carbohydrates: 30g | Protein: 30g | Fiber: 8g | Sodium: 600g

Chicken Sausage and Vegetable Skillet

Prep: 10 minutes | Cook: 20 minutes | Serves: 2

Ingredients:

- 2 chicken sausages, sliced (200g)
- 1 cup bell pepper, diced (150g)
- 1 cup zucchini, diced (124g)
- 1 Tbsp olive oil (15ml)
- 1/2 tsp garlic powder (1.5g)
- Salt and pepper to taste
- 1/4 tsp dried thyme (0.5g)
- 1/2 cup cherry tomatoes, halved (75g)

Instructions:

1. Heat olive oil in a large skillet over medium heat.
2. Add the sliced chicken sausages and cook until browned, about 5 minutes.
3. Add the diced bell pepper and zucchini to the skillet. Season with garlic powder, salt, pepper, and thyme. Cook, stirring occasionally, until the vegetables are tender, about 10 minutes.
4. Stir in the cherry tomatoes and cook for an additional 5 minutes, or until the tomatoes are soft and the sausage is cooked through.
5. Serve the skillet meal hot, directly from the skillet.

Nutritional Facts (Per Serving): Calories: 400 | Sugars: 6g | Fat: 22g | Carbohydrates: 20g | Protein: 32g | Fiber: 5g | Sodium: 800g

Greek Yogurt and Mixed Berry Parfait

Prep: 5 minutes | Cook: 0 minutes | Serves: 2

Ingredients:

- 1 cup Greek yogurt (245g)
- 1 cup mixed berries (strawberries, blueberries, raspberries) (140g)
- 1/4 cup granola (30g)
- 2 Tbsp honey (40ml)
- 1 Tbsp chia seeds (10g)

Instructions:

1. In two glasses or parfait cups, layer half of the Greek yogurt at the bottom.
2. Add a layer of mixed berries over the yogurt.
3. Sprinkle half of the granola over the berries and drizzle with 1 Tbsp of honey.
4. Add another layer of the remaining Greek yogurt, followed by the remaining berries, and top with the rest of the granola.
5. Drizzle the remaining honey over the top and sprinkle with chia seeds.
6. Serve immediately or refrigerate until ready to serve.

Nutritional Facts (Per Serving): Calories: 400 | Sugars: 35g | Fat: 10g | Carbohydrates: 60g | Protein: 20g | Fiber: 6g | Sodium: 50g

Beef and Spinach Breakfast Hash

Prep: 10 minutes | Cook: 20 minutes | Serves: 2

Ingredients:

- 1/2 lb lean ground beef (225g)
- 2 cups spinach, roughly chopped (60g)
- 1 medium potato, diced (150g)
- 1/2 tsp garlic powder (1.5g)
- Salt and pepper to taste
- 1/4 tsp paprika (0.5g)
- 1 small onion, diced (70g)
- 1 Tbsp olive oil (15ml)

Instructions:

1. Heat olive oil in a large skillet over medium heat.
2. Add the diced potato and onion, cooking until the potatoes are golden brown and the onions are translucent.
3. Add the ground beef to the skillet, breaking it apart with a spoon. Cook until the beef is browned.
4. Stir in the spinach, garlic powder, paprika, salt, and pepper. Cook until the spinach is wilted.
5. Serve the hash hot, divided between two plates.

Nutritional Facts (Per Serving): Calories: 400 | Sugars: 3g | Fat: 22g | Carbohydrates: 25g | Protein: 28g | Fiber: 3g | Sodium: 200g

Egg and Turkey Bacon Muffins

Prep: 10 minutes | Cook: 20 minutes | Serves: 4

Ingredients:

- 8 large eggs (440g)
- 4 slices turkey bacon, cooked and crumbled (120g)
- 1/2 cup shredded low-fat cheese (50g)
- 1/2 cup diced bell pepper (75g)
- Salt and pepper to taste
- 1 Tbsp chopped fresh chives (3g)
- 1/4 cup milk (60ml)

Instructions:

1. Preheat the oven to 375°F (190°C). Grease a muffin tin with cooking spray.
2. In a bowl, whisk together the eggs, milk, salt, and pepper.
3. Stir in the crumbled turkey bacon, shredded cheese, diced bell pepper, and chives.
4. Pour the mixture into the muffin cups, filling each about 3/4 full.
5. Bake for 18-20 minutes, or until the egg muffins are set and lightly golden on top.
6. Let cool for a few minutes before serving.

Nutritional Facts (Per Serving): Calories: 400 | Sugars: 3g | Fat: 24g | Carbohydrates: 5g | Protein: 38g | Fiber: 1g | Sodium: 600g

Protein-Packed Breakfast Tacos

Prep: 10 minutes | Cook: 10 minutes | Serves: 2

Ingredients:

- 4 small whole wheat tortillas (200g total)
- 6 large eggs (330g)
- 1/2 cup black beans, drained and rinsed (90g)
- 1/2 cup shredded cheddar cheese (50g)
- 1 avocado, sliced (200g)
- 1/4 cup salsa (60g)
- 2 Tbsp olive oil (30ml)
- Salt and pepper to taste
- 1/4 tsp cumin (0.5g)
- 1/4 cup fresh cilantro, chopped (4g)

Instructions:

1. Beat the eggs in a bowl. Stir in the black beans, cumin, salt, and pepper.
2. Heat 1 tablespoon of olive oil in a skillet over medium heat. Pour in the egg mixture, cooking and stirring until the eggs are set, about 3-4 minutes.
3. Warm the tortillas in a separate pan or in the microwave for about 10 seconds each.
4. Divide the cooked egg mixture among the tortillas.
5. Top each taco with shredded cheese, avocado slices, and salsa.
6. Garnish with fresh cilantro and serve immediately.

Nutritional Facts (Per Serving): Calories: 400 | Sugars: 4g | Fat: 24g | Carbohydrates: 28g | Protein: 24g | Fiber: 7g | Sodium: 700g

CHAPTER 5: BREAKFASTS
Revitalizing Smoothies: A Blend of Health and Flavor

Crete Avocado and Pineapple Creaminess

Prep: 5 minutes | Cook: 0 minutes | Serves: 2

Ingredients:

- 1 ripe avocado, pitted and scooped (200g)
- 1 cup pineapple chunks (165g)
- 1/2 cup Greek yogurt (120g)
- 2 Tbsp honey (40ml)

Instructions:

1. Combine avocado, pineapple chunks, Greek yogurt, and honey in a blender.
2. Blend until smooth and creamy.
3. Divide the mixture into two bowls or glasses and serve immediately.

Nutritional Facts (Per Serving): 400 | Sugars: 35g | Fat: 20g | Carbohydrates: 52g | Protein: 8g | Fiber: 7g | Sodium: 30g

Rhodes Raspberry and Oat Fuel

Prep: 5 minutes | Cook: 0 minutes | Serves: 2

Ingredients:

- 1 cup raspberries (123g)
- 1/2 cup rolled oats (40g)
- 1 cup almond milk (240ml)
- 1 scoop protein powder (30g, depending on brand)

Instructions:

1. Place raspberries, rolled oats, almond milk, and protein powder in a blender.
Blend until smooth.
Serve immediately, optionally topped with a few whole raspberries or a sprinkle of oats.

Nutritional Facts (Per Serving): Calories: 400 | Sugars: 12g | Fat: 8g | Carbohydrates: 58g | Protein: 24g | Fiber: 10g | Sodium: 150g

Sicilian Almond and Banana Powerhouse

Prep: 5 minutes | Cook: 0 minutes | Serves: 2

Ingredients:

- 2 ripe bananas (240g)
- 2 Tbsp almond butter (32g)
- 1 cup whole milk (240ml)
- 1 Tbsp chia seeds (10g)

Instructions:

1. Add bananas, almond butter, and whole milk to a blender.
2. Blend until smooth.
3. Pour into glasses and sprinkle chia seeds on top.
4. Serve immediately or let sit for a few minutes to allow chia seeds to swell.

Nutritional Facts (Per Serving): Calories: 400 | Sugars: 30g | Fat: 18g | Carbohydrates: 50g | Protein: 12g | Fiber: 7g | Sodium: 80g

Ionian Island Kiwi and Spinach Zest

Prep: 5 minutes | Cook: 0 minutes | Serves: 2

Ingredients:

- 3 ripe kiwis, peeled and sliced (270g)
- 1 cup fresh spinach leaves (30g)
- 1/2 cup Greek yogurt (120g)
- 1/2 cup orange juice (120ml)

Instructions:

1. Place kiwi slices, spinach leaves, Greek yogurt, and orange juice in a blender.
2. Blend until smooth and creamy.
3. Divide the mixture between two glasses and serve immediately for a refreshing and nutritious boost.

Nutritional Facts (Per Serving): Calories: 400 | Sugars: 28g | Fat: 2g | Carbohydrates: 76g | Protein: 16g | Fiber: 5g | Sodium: 45g

CHAPTER 6: BREAKFASTS
Revitalizing Smoothies: A Blend of Health and Flavor

Berry Barley Breakfast Bowl

Prep: 5 minutes (plus overnight soaking) | Cook: 20 minutes | Serves: 2

Ingredients:

- 1 cup hulled barley, soaked overnight (200g)
- 2 cups water (480ml)
- 1/2 cup mixed berries (fresh or frozen) (70g)
- 1/4 cup chopped nuts (almonds, walnuts) (30g)
- 2 Tbsp honey (40ml)
- 1/2 cup Greek yogurt (120g)

Instructions:

1. Drain and rinse the soaked barley. In a saucepan, combine barley with water and bring to a boil. Reduce heat, cover, and simmer for 20 minutes or until tender.
Divide the cooked barley between two bowls.
Top with mixed berries, chopped nuts, and a drizzle of honey.
Add a dollop of Greek yogurt to each bowl before serving.

Nutritional Facts (Per Serving): Calories: 400 | Sugars: 18g | Fat: 10g | Carbohydrates: 68g | Protein: 14g | Fiber: 15g | Sodium: 30g

Banana Almond Oatmeal

Prep: 5 minutes | Cook: 10 minutes | Serves: 2

Ingredients:

- 1 cup rolled oats (80g)
- 2 cups almond milk (480ml)
- 1 ripe banana, mashed (100g)
- 2 Tbsp almond butter (32g)
- 1 Tbsp chia seeds (10g)
- 1/2 tsp cinnamon (1g)

Instructions:

1. In a saucepan, bring the almond milk to a boil. Add the oats and reduce heat to a simmer.
2. Cook for 5-7 minutes, stirring occasionally, until the oats are soft.
3. Remove from heat and stir in the mashed banana, almond butter, chia seeds, and cinnamon.
4. Divide the oatmeal between two bowls and serve.

Nutritional Facts (Per Serving): Calories: 400 | Sugars: 12g | Fat: 18g | Carbohydrates: 52g | Protein: 12g | Fiber: 9g | Sodium: 150g

Spiced Pumpkin Quinoa Breakfast Bowl

Prep: 5 minutes | Cook: 20 minutes | Serves: 2

Ingredients:

- 1/2 cup quinoa (85g)
- 1 cup canned pumpkin puree (245g)
- 1 1/2 cups almond milk (360ml)
- 1 tsp pumpkin pie spice (2g)
- 2 Tbsp maple syrup (30ml)
- 1/4 cup pecans, chopped (30g)

Instructions:

1. Rinse quinoa under cold water. In a saucepan, combine quinoa, pumpkin puree, almond milk, and pumpkin pie spice. Bring to a boil.
2. Reduce heat to low, cover, and simmer for 15-20 minutes, or until quinoa is cooked and most of the liquid is absorbed.
3. Stir in the maple syrup.
4. Divide the quinoa mixture between two bowls and top with chopped pecans before serving.

Nutritional Facts (Per Serving): Calories: 400 | Sugars: 18g | Fat: 14g | Carbohydrates: 62g | Protein: 10g | Fiber: 8g | Sodium: 80g

Apricot and Hazelnut Bulgur

Prep: 10 minutes | Cook: 15 minutes | Serves: 2

Ingredients:

- 1 cup bulgur (182g)
- 2 cups water (480ml)
- 1/2 cup dried apricots, chopped (90g)
- 1/4 cup hazelnuts, toasted and chopped (34g)
- 1 Tbsp honey (21g)
- 1/2 tsp cinnamon (1g)
- 1/4 tsp salt (1.5g)
- Zest of 1 orange

Instructions:

1. In a medium saucepan, bring water to a boil. Add bulgur and salt, then reduce heat to low. Cover and simmer for 12-15 minutes until the bulgur is tender and the water is absorbed.
2. Stir in the chopped apricots, toasted hazelnuts, honey, cinnamon, and orange zest into the cooked bulgur.
3. Mix well and let it sit for 5 minutes to allow the flavors to meld.
4. Serve warm, or allow to cool and serve at room temperature.

Nutritional Facts (Per Serving): Calories: 400 | Sugars: 20g | Fat: 12g | Carbohydrates: 68g | Protein: 10g | Fiber: 12g | Sodium: 300

CHAPTER 7: LUNCHES
Satisfying Soups and Stews: The Heart of Mediterranean Cuisine

Provencal Vegetable Soup with Pesto

Prep: 15 minutes | Cook: 30 minutes | Serves: 4

Ingredients:

- 2 tbsp olive oil (30 ml)
- 1 large onion, chopped (150g)
- 2 cloves garlic, minced
- 2 large carrots, diced (150g)
- 1 large zucchini, diced (150g)
- 1 red bell pepper, diced (150g)
- 4 cups vegetable broth (950 ml)
- 2 large tomatoes, diced (200g)
- 2 tbsp pesto (30 ml)
- Salt and pepper to taste

Instructions:

1. Heat olive oil in a pot over medium heat. Sauté onion and garlic until translucent.
2. Add carrots, zucchini, and bell pepper; cook for 5 minutes.
3. Add broth and tomatoes; simmer for 20 minutes. Stir in pesto; season with salt and pepper. Serve hot.

Nutritional Facts (Per Serving): Calories: 500 | Sugars: 12g | Fat: 22g | Carbohydrates: 68g | Protein: 14g | Fiber: 10g | Sodium: 800mg

Lentil Soup with Vegetables and Thyme

Prep: 10 minutes | Cook: 45 minutes | Serves: 4

Ingredients:

- 1 cup lentils (200g), rinsed
- 1 carrot (100g), diced
- 1 onion (70g), diced
- 2 celery stalks (80g), diced
- 2 cloves garlic, minced
- 1 can diced tomatoes (14 oz or 400g)
- 4 cups vegetable broth (950ml)
- 1 tsp thyme (1g)
- 2 Tbsp olive oil (30ml)
- Salt and pepper to taste

Instructions:

1. In a large pot, heat olive oil over medium heat. Add onion, carrot, celery, and garlic. Sauté until vegetables are softened.
2. Add lentils, diced tomatoes, vegetable broth, thyme, salt, and pepper. Bring to a boil.
3. Reduce heat and simmer for about 35 minutes, or until lentils are tender.
4. Adjust seasoning to taste. Serve hot.

Nutritional Facts (Per Serving): Calories: 500 | Sugars: 8g | Fat: 10g | Carbohydrates: 80g | Protein: 25g | Fiber: 20g | Sodium: 400mg

Andalusian Gazpacho with Almonds

Prep: 20 minutes | Cook: 0 minutes | Serves: 4

Ingredients:

- 6 large ripe tomatoes, peeled and chopped (1kg)
- 1 cucumber, peeled and chopped (250g)
- 1 green bell pepper, chopped (150g)
- 1 small onion, chopped (100g)
- 2 cloves garlic
- 1/3 cup blanched almonds (45g)
- 3 tbsp olive oil (45 ml)
- 2 tbsp red wine vinegar (30 ml)
- Salt and pepper to taste
- 2 cups cold water (475 ml)

Instructions:

1. Blend all ingredients until smooth.
2. Chill for at least 2 hours.
3. Adjust seasoning; serve cold.

Nutritional Facts (Per Serving): Calories: 500 | Sugars: 15g | Fat: 35g | Carbohydrates: 40g | Protein: 10g | Fiber: 9g | Sodium: 250mg

Greek Lemon Chicken Orzo Soup

Prep: 15 minutes | Cook: 40 minutes | Serves: 4

Ingredients:

- 2 tbsp olive oil (30 ml)
- 1 large onion, chopped (150g)
- 2 carrots, diced (150g)
- 2 stalks celery, diced (150g)
- 10 oz chicken breast, diced (280g)
- 6 cups chicken broth (1.4 liters)
- 2/3 cup orzo (120g)
- Juice and zest of 2 lemons
- 2 tbsp fresh dill, chopped (30 ml)
- Salt and pepper to taste

Instructions:

1. Sauté onion, carrots, and celery in oil.
2. Add chicken; brown slightly.
3. Add broth and orzo; cook until orzo is tender.
4. Stir in lemon juice, zest, and dill; season.
5. Serve hot.

Nutritional Facts (Per Serving): Calories: 500 | Sugars: 6g | Fat: 15g | Carbohydrates: 52g | Protein: 35g | Fiber: 4g | Sodium: 950mg

Turkish Beef and Eggplant Stew

Prep: 20 minutes | Cook: 1 hour | Serves: 4

Ingredients:

- 1 lb beef, cubed (450g)
- 2 eggplants, cubed (600g)
- 1 onion, chopped (150g)
- 2 tomatoes, diced (200g)
- 3 cups beef broth (700 ml)
- 1 tsp cumin (5 ml)
- 1/2 tsp cinnamon (2.5 ml)
- Salt and pepper to taste
- 2 tbsp olive oil (30 ml)

Instructions:

1. Brown beef in olive oil. Remove and set aside.
2. In the same pot, sauté onion and eggplant until soft.
3. Return beef to the pot, add tomatoes, broth, cumin, and cinnamon.
4. Simmer until beef is tender, about 45 minutes.
5. Season with salt and pepper. Serve hot.

Nutritional Facts (Per Serving): Calories: 500 | Sugars: 10g | Fat: 30g | Carbohydrates: 30g | Protein: 35g | Fiber: 8g | Sodium: 600mg

Moroccan Lamb Tagine

Prep: 20 minutes | Cook: 2 hours | Serves: 4

Ingredients:

- 1 lb lamb shoulder, cubed (450g)
- 1 onion, finely chopped (150g)
- 2 cloves garlic, minced
- 1 cup dried apricots, chopped (130g)
- 1/4 cup almonds, toasted (30g)
- 2 cups beef or chicken broth (475 ml)
- 1 tsp ground cumin (5 ml)
- 1 tsp ground cinnamon (5 ml)
- 1 tsp ground ginger (5 ml)
- 2 tbsp olive oil (30 ml)
- Salt and pepper to taste
- 2 cups couscous, cooked (340g)

Instructions:

1. In a tagine or heavy pot, heat olive oil and brown the lamb.
2. Add onions and garlic, cook until softened.
3. Stir in spices, apricots, almonds, and broth. Bring to a simmer.
4. Cover and cook on low heat for 1.5 to 2 hours until lamb is tender.
5. Serve over couscous.

Nutritional Facts (Per Serving): Calories: 500 | Sugars: 20g | Fat: 15g | Carbohydrates: 60g | Protein: 35g | Fiber: 5g | Sodium: 600mg

Italian Pork Ragu with Porcini Mushrooms

Prep: 20 minutes | Cook: 2 hours | Serves: 4

Ingredients:

- 1 lb pork shoulder, cubed (450g)
- 1 oz dried porcini mushrooms (30g)
- 1 cup beef broth (240 ml)
- 1 onion, finely chopped (150g)
- 2 garlic cloves, minced
- 1 can crushed tomatoes (28 oz, 800g)
- 1 tbsp tomato paste (15 ml)
- 1/2 cup red wine (120 ml)
- 2 tbsp olive oil (30 ml)
- 1 tsp dried thyme (5 ml)
- Salt and pepper to taste
- Fresh parsley, chopped for garnish

Instructions:

1. Soak porcini mushrooms in beef broth to rehydrate. Set aside.

2. Brown pork in olive oil over medium heat. Remove and set aside.

3. Sauté onion and garlic in the same pot. Add tomato paste, cook for 1 minute.

4. Pour in red wine, cook until reduced by half.

5. Add crushed tomatoes, thyme, pork, and porcini with broth. Simmer for 2 hours.

6. Season with salt and pepper, garnish with parsley. Serve over pasta or polenta.

Nutritional Facts (Per Serving): Calories: 500 | Sugars: 6g | Fat: 30g | Carbohydrates: 20g | Protein: 35g | Fiber: 3g | Sodium: 600mg

Hearty Provencal Lamb Stew with Herbes de Provence

Prep: 20 minutes | Cook: 2 hours | Serves: 4

Ingredients:

- 1 lb lamb leg or shoulder, cubed (450g)
- 1 onion, chopped (150g)
- 2 carrots, sliced (100g)
- 2 cups chicken stock (475 ml)
- 1/2 cup white wine (120 ml)
- 2 tbsp olive oil (30 ml)
- 2 tbsp Herbes de Provence (30 ml)
- Salt and pepper to taste
- 1 bay leaf

Instructions:

1. Sear lamb in olive oil until browned. Remove from pot.

2. Sauté onion and carrots in the same pot. Deglaze with wine.

3. Return lamb to pot, add stock, Herbes de Provence, bay leaf, salt, and pepper.

4. Cover, simmer for 1.5 to 2 hours until lamb is tender.

5. Adjust seasoning and serve with crusty bread.

Nutritional Facts (Per Serving): Calories: 500 | Sugars: 5g | Fat: 25g | Carbohydrates: 15g | Protein: 40g | Fiber: 3g | Sodium: 500mg

CHAPTER 8: LUNCHES
Wholesome Pasta and Grains: Fast, Fresh, and Full of Flavor

Pasta Puttanesca

Prep: 10 minutes | Cook: 20 minutes | Serves: 4

Ingredients:

- 12 oz spaghetti (340g)
- 2 tbsp olive oil (30 ml)
- 4 anchovy fillets, chopped (20g)
- 3 cloves garlic, minced
- 1/2 cup pitted Kalamata olives, sliced (75g)
- 2 tbsp capers, drained (30 ml)
- 1 can crushed tomatoes (28 oz, 794g)
- 1 tsp red pepper flakes (5 ml)
- Salt and pepper to taste
- Fresh parsley, chopped for garnish

Instructions:

1. Cook spaghetti in salted boiling water until al dente; drain and set aside.
2. In a large pan, heat olive oil over medium heat. Add anchovies and garlic, cook until fragrant.
3. Stir in olives, capers, and red pepper flakes; sauté for a few minutes.
4. Pour in crushed tomatoes, season with salt and pepper. Simmer for 15 minutes.
5. Toss the spaghetti with the sauce, heat through.
6. Garnish with fresh parsley before serving.

Nutritional Facts (Per Serving): Calories: 500 | Sugars: 8g | Fat: 10g | Carbohydrates: 80g | Protein: 20g | Fiber: 6g | Sodium: 800mg

Spaghetti Carbonara

Prep: 10 minutes | Cook: 20 minutes | Serves: 4

Ingredients:

- 12 oz tagliatelle pasta (340g)
- 4 large eggs
- 2 cups fresh spinach (60g)
- 1 cup cherry tomatoes, halved (150g)
- 4 slices bacon, cut into pieces (120g)
- 1/4 cup grated Parmesan cheese, plus extra for garnish (25g)
- 2 tbsp olive oil (30 ml)
- Salt and pepper to taste
- A pinch of red pepper flakes

Instructions:

1. Cook tagliatelle al dente according to package instructions. Reserve 1/2 cup of pasta water before draining (120 ml).
2. In a pot, soft-boil the eggs for 6-7 minutes, then place in ice water before peeling.
3. In a skillet, cook bacon over medium heat until crispy, then set aside on paper towels.
4. In the same skillet, add olive oil, cherry tomatoes, and spinach. Sauté until spinach wilts.
5. Toss the cooked pasta with the vegetables, adding pasta water to create a light sauce.
5. Slice the soft-boiled eggs in half.
6. Plate the pasta, top with bacon pieces, Parmesan cheese, egg halves, a sprinkle of red pepper flakes, and season with salt and pepper.
7. Serve with additional grated Parmesan on the side.

Nutritional Facts (Per Serving): Calories: 500 | Sugars: 3g | Fat: 15g | Carbohydrates: 65g | Protein: 25g | Fiber: 3g | Sodium: 600mg

Farfalle with Spinach Pesto and Pine Nuts

Prep: 15 minutes | Cook: 10 minutes | Serves: 4

Ingredients:

- 12 oz farfalle pasta (340g)
- 2 cups fresh spinach (60g)
- 1/2 cup pine nuts (70g), plus extra for garnish
- 1/4 cup grated Parmesan cheese (25g)
- 2 cloves garlic
- 1/2 cup olive oil (120ml)
- Salt and pepper to taste

Instructions:

1. Cook farfalle according to package instructions.
2. Drain, reserving 1 cup (240ml) of pasta water, and set aside.
3. In a food processor, blend spinach, pine nuts, Parmesan cheese, and garlic until smooth. Gradually add olive oil until you achieve a smooth pesto.
4. Toss cooked farfalle with the spinach pesto, adding reserved pasta water as needed to achieve desired consistency.
5. Season with salt and pepper to taste. Serve garnished with extra pine nuts.

Nutritional Facts (Per Serving): Calories: 500 | Sugars: 3g | Fat: 25g | Carbohydrates: 60g | Protein: 15g | Fiber: 5g | Sodium: 200mg

Penne Arrabbiata with Olives

Prep: 10 minutes | Cook: 20 minutes | Serves: 4

Ingredients:

- 12 oz penne pasta (340g)
- 2 cups tomato sauce (480ml)
- 1/2 cup black olives (80g), pitted and sliced
- 1 tsp red pepper flakes (2g)
- 2 Tbsp olive oil (30ml)
- Salt to taste
- Fresh basil for garnish
- 2 cloves garlic, minced

Instructions:

1. Cook penne according to package instructions.
2. Drain and set aside.
3. Heat olive oil in a large pan over medium heat. Add garlic and red pepper flakes, sauté for 1 minute.
4. Add tomato sauce and olives. Simmer for 10 minutes.
5. Toss the cooked penne in the sauce. Season with salt.
6. Garnish with fresh basil before serving.

Nutritional Facts (Per Serving): Calories: 500 | Sugars: 6g | Fat: 10g | Carbohydrates: 85g | Protein: 15g | Fiber: 5g | Sodium: 400mg

Orzo with Grilled Vegetables and Feta Cheese

Prep: 15 minutes | Cook: 20 minutes | Serves: 4

Ingredients:

- 1 cup orzo (200g)
- 1 zucchini (150g), sliced
- 1 bell pepper (150g), sliced
- 1/2 cup cherry tomatoes (75g), halved
- 1/2 cup feta cheese (75g), crumbled
- 2 Tbsp olive oil (30ml), plus more for grilling
- Juice of 1 lemon
- Salt and pepper to taste
- Fresh herbs (parsley, basil) for garnish

Instructions:

1. Cook orzo according to package instructions. Drain and set aside.
2. Preheat grill to medium-high. Brush zucchini and bell pepper with olive oil. Grill until tender and slightly charred.
3. In a large bowl, combine cooked orzo, grilled vegetables, cherry tomatoes, feta cheese, olive oil, and lemon juice. Season with salt and pepper.
4. Garnish with fresh herbs before serving.

Nutritional Facts (Per Serving): Calories: 500 | Sugars: 5g | Fat: 15g | Carbohydrates: 75g | Protein: 15g | Fiber: 5g | Sodium: 300mg

Tortellini with Spinach and Walnut Pesto

Prep: 15 minutes | Cook: 10 minutes | Serves: 4

Ingredients:

- 1 lb fresh tortellini (450g)
- 2 cups fresh spinach (60g)
- 1/2 cup walnuts (60g)
- 2 cloves garlic
- 1/4 cup olive oil (60ml)
- Salt and pepper to taste
- 1/4 cup grated Parmesan cheese (25g)

Instructions:

1. Cook tortellini according to package instructions.
2. Drain and set aside.
3. In a food processor, blend spinach, walnuts, Parmesan cheese, garlic, and olive oil until smooth.
4. Season with salt and pepper.
5. Toss cooked tortellini with the spinach and walnut pesto.
6. Serve immediately, garnished with extra Parmesan if desired.

Nutritional Facts (Per Serving): Calories: 500 | Sugars: 3g | Fat: 25g | Carbohydrates: 50g | Protein: 20g | Fiber: 4g | Sodium: 600mg

Pasta with Chicken, Artichokes, and Cream Sauce

Prep: 15 minutes | Cook: 20 minutes | Serves: 4

Ingredients:

- 8 oz pasta (225g), any shape
- 1 lb chicken breast (450g), cubed
- 1 can artichoke hearts (14 oz or 400g), drained and quartered
- 1 cup heavy cream (240ml)
- 2 cloves garlic, minced
- 1/4 cup grated Parmesan cheese (25g)
- 2 Tbsp olive oil (30ml)
- Salt and pepper to taste
- Fresh parsley for garnish
- 1 onion (70g), finely chopped

Instructions:

1. Cook pasta according to package instructions. Drain and set aside.

2. Heat olive oil in a large skillet over medium heat. Add chicken, season with salt and pepper, and cook until browned and cooked through. Remove and set aside.

3. In the same skillet, add onion and garlic. Sauté until soft.

4. Add artichoke hearts and heavy cream. Bring to a simmer.

5. Return chicken to the skillet. Add cooked pasta and Parmesan cheese. Toss until everything is well coated and heated through.

6. Season with salt and pepper to taste. Garnish with fresh parsley before serving.

Nutritional Facts (Per Serving): Calories: 500 | Sugars: 4g | Fat: 22g | Carbohydrates: 45g | Protein: 30g | Fiber: 3g | Sodium: 400mg

Pesto Penne with Roasted Cherry Tomatoes and Almonds

Prep: 10 minutes | Cook: 20 minutes | Serves: 4

Ingredients:

- 12 oz penne pasta (340g)
- 2 cups fresh basil leaves (80g)
- 1/3 cup grated Parmesan cheese (35g)
- 1/4 cup pine nuts (30g), plus a handful of whole almonds for garnish
- 2 garlic cloves
- 1/2 cup olive oil (120 ml), plus extra for drizzling
- 1 cup cherry tomatoes, halved (150g)
- Salt and pepper to taste
- Shavings of Parmesan cheese, for garnish

Instructions:

1. Preheat oven to 400°F (200°C). Toss cherry tomatoes with a drizzle of olive oil, salt, and pepper.

2. Roast for 15-20 minutes until burst and caramelized.

3. Cook penne according to package instructions until al dente; drain, reserving a cup of pasta water.

4. For the pesto, blend basil leaves, grated Parmesan, pine nuts, garlic, and olive oil until smooth, seasoning with salt and pepper to taste.

5. Toss the penne with pesto, adding pasta water as needed to loosen the sauce.

6. Serve the pasta topped with roasted cherry

tomatoes, almond garnish, and Parmesan shavings.

7. Drizzle with a touch more olive oil and a grind of fresh pepper before serving.

Nutritional Facts (Per Serving): Calories: 500 | Sugars: 4g | Fat: 28g | Carbohydrates: 50g | Protein: 15g | Fiber: 4g | Sodium: 300mg

Lasagna with Vegetables and Ricotta

Prep: 20 minutes | Cook: 45 minutes | Serves: 6

Ingredients:

- 9 lasagna noodles (270g)
- 1 cup ricotta cheese (250g)
- 1 zucchini, thinly sliced (150g)
- 1 eggplant, thinly sliced (200g)
- 1 bell pepper, thinly sliced (150g)
- 1 cup shredded mozzarella cheese (100g)
- 2 cups tomato sauce (480ml)
- 2 Tbsp olive oil (30ml)
- 1 tsp salt (5g)
- 1/2 tsp black pepper (2g)
- 2 cups spinach (60g)

Instructions:

1. Preheat oven to 375°F (190°C).
2. Sauté zucchini, eggplant, and bell pepper in olive oil until slightly tender. Season with salt and pepper.
3. Spread a thin layer of tomato sauce in the bottom of a baking dish.

4. Layer 3 lasagna noodles, followed by half of the vegetable mixture, spinach, ricotta, and a sprinkle of mozzarella.
5. Repeat with another layer of noodles, vegetables, spinach, ricotta, and mozzarella.
6. Top with the final layer of noodles, remaining tomato sauce, and mozzarella.
7. Cover with foil and bake for 30 minutes. Remove foil and bake for an additional 15 minutes until cheese is golden.
8. Let stand for 10 minutes before serving.

Nutritional Facts (Per Serving): Calories: 500 | Sugars: 8g | Fat: 18g | Carbohydrates: 58g | Protein: 25g | Fiber: 6g | Sodium: 800mg

Pizza Margherita

Prep: 15 minutes (plus dough) | Cook: 10 minutes | Serves: 4

Ingredients:

- 1 lb pizza dough (450g)
- 1 cup tomato sauce (240 ml)
- 1 cup shredded mozzarella cheese (100g)
- Fresh basil leaves
- 2 tbsp olive oil (30 ml)
- Salt to taste

Instructions:

1. Roll out pizza dough, spread tomato sauce, sprinkle with cheese.
2. Bake at 475°F (245°C) for 10 minutes until crust is golden.
3. Garnish with basil and a drizzle of olive oil.

Nutritional Facts (Per Serving): Calories: 500 | Sugars: 5g | Fat: 20g | Carbohydrates: 60g | Protein: 20g | Fiber: 3g | Sodium: 800mg

CHAPTER 9: LUNCHES
Mediterranean Risotto: Creamy, Comforting, and Nutrient-Rich

Asparagus and Lemon Zest Risotto

Prep: 10 minutes | Cook: 25 minutes | Serves: 4

Ingredients:

- 1 lb asparagus (450g), trimmed and cut into 1-inch pieces
- 1 1/2 cups Arborio rice (300g)
- 4 cups vegetable broth (950ml)
- 1 onion (70g), finely chopped
- 2 Tbsp olive oil (30ml)
- Zest of 1 lemon
- 1/2 cup grated Parmesan cheese (45g)
- Salt and pepper to taste

Instructions:

1. In a saucepan, bring the vegetable broth to a simmer.
2. In another pan, heat olive oil over medium heat.
3. Sauté onion until translucent.
4. Add Arborio rice and cook for 1-2 minutes, stirring frequently.
5. Gradually add warm broth one cup at a time, allowing the rice to absorb the liquid before adding more. Stir constantly.
6. Halfway through, add the asparagus. Continue to add broth and stir until the rice is creamy and asparagus is tender.
7. Remove from heat. Stir in lemon zest and Parmesan cheese. Season with salt and pepper.
8. Serve immediately.

Nutritional Facts (Per Serving): Calories: 500 | Sugars: 4g | Fat: 12g | Carbohydrates: 80g | Protein: 15g | Fiber: 5g | Sodium: 400mg

Tomato Basil Risotto with Mozzarella

Prep: 10 minutes | Cook: 25 minutes | Serves: 4

Ingredients:

- 1 1/2 cups Arborio rice (300g)
- 4 cups vegetable broth (950ml)
- 1 can diced tomatoes (14 oz or 400g)
- 1 onion (70g), finely chopped
- 2 cloves garlic, minced
- 1 cup fresh basil (40g), chopped
- 1/2 cup mozzarella cheese (50g), diced
- 2 Tbsp olive oil (30ml)
- Salt and pepper to taste

Instructions:

1. In a saucepan, keep vegetable broth warm over low heat.
2. In a large pan, heat olive oil over medium heat.
3. Add onion and garlic, sauté until soft.
4. Add Arborio rice, cooking for 1-2 minutes until slightly toasted.
5. Start adding warm broth one cup at a time, stirring until each addition is absorbed before adding the next.
6. Halfway through, stir in diced tomatoes. Continue cooking and adding broth as before.
7. Once the rice is creamy and cooked, remove from heat. Stir in basil and mozzarella. Season with salt and pepper.
8. Serve immediately, garnished with additional basil if desired.

Nutritional Facts (Per Serving): Calories: 500 | Sugars: 6g | Fat: 12g | Carbohydrates: 80g | Protein: 15g | Fiber: 3g | Sodium: 500mg

Risotto with Grilled Eggplant and Balsamic

Prep: 15 minutes | Cook: 30 minutes | Serves: 4

Ingredients:

- 1 eggplant (300g), sliced and grilled
- 1 1/2 cups Arborio rice (300g)
- 4 cups vegetable broth (950ml)
- 1 onion (70g), finely chopped
- 2 Tbsp olive oil (30ml)
- 1/4 cup balsamic vinegar (60ml)
- 1/2 cup grated Parmesan cheese (45g)
- Salt and pepper to taste

Instructions:

1. Preheat grill. Brush eggplant slices with olive oil and grill until tender. Cut into cubes and set aside.

2. In a saucepan, keep vegetable broth warm over low heat.

3. In another pan, heat olive oil over medium heat.

4. Sauté onion until translucent.

5. Add Arborio rice, stirring for 1-2 minutes until slightly toasted.

6. Gradually add broth one cup at a time, stirring continuously until liquid is absorbed before adding more.

7. Near the end of cooking, stir in grilled eggplant and balsamic vinegar. Continue to cook until rice is creamy.

8. Remove from heat, stir in Parmesan cheese. Season with salt and pepper.

9. Serve immediately, garnished with additional Parmesan if desired.

Nutritional Facts (Per Serving): Calories: 500 | Sugars: 8g | Fat: 12g | Carbohydrates: 80g | Protein: 15g | Fiber: 5g | Sodium: 400mg

Pumpkin and Gorgonzola Risotto

Prep: 10 minutes | Cook: 30 minutes | Serves: 4

Ingredients:

- 1 cup Arborio rice (200g)
- 2 cups pumpkin, cubed (300g)
- 4 cups vegetable stock (950 ml)
- 1 onion, finely chopped (150g)
- 1/2 cup white wine (120 ml)
- 4 oz Gorgonzola cheese, crumbled (115g)
- 2 tbsp olive oil (30 ml)
- Salt and pepper to taste
- Fresh sage, chopped for garnish

Instructions:

1. Sauté onion in olive oil until translucent. Add rice, cook until slightly toasted.

2. Stir in pumpkin, then add wine, cook until absorbed.

3. Gradually add stock, stirring continuously until rice is al dente and pumpkin is soft.

4. Stir in Gorgonzola, season with salt and pepper.
5. Garnish with sage. Serve immediately.

Nutritional Facts (Per Serving): Calories: 500 | Sugars: 6g | Fat: 20g | Carbohydrates: 65g | Protein: 15g | Fiber: 3g | Sodium: 700mg

Seafood Paella

Prep: 20 minutes | Cook: 40 minutes | Serves: 4

Ingredients:

- 1 cup short-grain paella rice (200g)
- 1 lb mixed seafood (shrimp, mussels, clams) (450g)
- 4 cups fish stock (950 ml)
- 1/2 cup canned diced tomatoes (120g)
- 1 bell pepper, sliced (150g)
- 1/2 cup frozen peas (75g)
- 1 onion, finely chopped (150g)
- 2 cloves garlic, minced
- 1 pinch saffron threads
- 2 tbsp olive oil (30 ml)
- Salt and pepper to taste
- 1 lemon, cut into wedges for serving

Instructions:

1. In a paella pan or large skillet, heat olive oil over medium heat. Sauté onions and garlic until translucent.
2. Add rice, stirring to coat with oil, cook for 2 minutes.
3. Add fish stock, saffron, and tomatoes. Bring to a simmer.

4. Arrange seafood on top. Cover and cook for 20-25 minutes until rice is cooked and seafood is done.
5. Add peas and bell peppers in the last 10 minutes.
6. Let it sit for 5 minutes off the heat before serving with lemon wedges.

Nutritional Facts (Per Serving): Calories: 500 | Sugars: 5g | Fat: 10g | Carbohydrates: 75g | Protein: 35g | Fiber: 4g | Sodium: 600mg

Risotto with Porcini Mushrooms and Thyme

Prep: 15 minutes | Cook: 30 minutes | Serves: 4

Ingredients:

- 1 cup Arborio rice (200g)
- 1 oz dried porcini mushrooms (30g)
- 4 cups vegetable broth (950 ml)
- 1 small onion, finely chopped (70g)
- 1/2 cup dry white wine (120 ml)
- 2 tbsp unsalted butter (30 ml)
- 2 tbsp fresh thyme leaves (30 ml)
- 1/4 cup grated Parmesan cheese (25g)
- Salt and freshly ground black pepper to taste
- 2 tbsp olive oil (30 ml)

Instructions:

1. Soak porcini mushrooms in warm water for 20 minutes, then chop.
2. Heat broth in a saucepan and keep warm.
3. In another pan, heat olive oil, add onion, and cook until translucent.
4. Stir in rice, cook for 1-2 minutes. Add wine, cook until absorbed.
5. Add mushrooms and thyme, then ladle in broth, stirring until each addition is absorbed.
6. Once rice is creamy and al dente, remove from heat, stir in butter and Parmesan.
7. Season with salt and pepper. Serve immediately.

Nutritional Facts (Per Serving): Calories: 500 | Sugars: 2g | Fat: 15g | Carbohydrates: 75g | Protein: 10g | Fiber: 3g | Sodium: 600mg

CHAPTER 10: LUNCHES
Mediterranean Meats: Tender, Herbed, and Savory

Grilled Lamb Chops with Rosemary and Garlic

Prep: 20 minutes (plus marinating) | Cook: 10 minutes | Serves: 4

Ingredients:

- 8 lamb chops (800g)
- 2 Tbsp olive oil (30ml)
- 4 cloves garlic, minced
- 2 Tbsp fresh rosemary (6g), chopped
- Salt and pepper to taste
- Garnish: Grilled asparagus (200g) and quinoa salad (1/2 cup cooked quinoa, 85g)

Instructions:

1. Mix olive oil, garlic, rosemary, salt, and pepper.
2. Marinate lamb chops for at least 1 hour in the refrigerator.
3. Preheat grill to medium-high heat. Grill lamb chops to desired doneness, about 3-4 minutes per side for medium-rare.
4. Grill asparagus alongside lamb chops until tender.
5. Serve lamb chops with grilled asparagus and a side of quinoa salad.

Nutritional Facts (Per Serving): Calories: 500 | Sugars: 2g | Fat: 25g | Carbohydrates: 20g | Protein: 50g | Fiber: 5g | Sodium: 200mg

Pork Souvlaki with Tzatziki

Prep: 25 minutes (plus marinating) | Cook: 10 minutes | Serves: 4

Ingredients:

- 1 lb pork tenderloin (450g), cubed
- 2 Tbsp olive oil (30ml)
- Juice of 1 lemon
- 2 cloves garlic, minced
- 1 tsp oregano (1g)
- Salt and pepper to taste
- Garnish: Greek salad (1 cup tomatoes (150g), 1 cup cucumbers (100g), 1/4 cup olives (30g), 2 oz feta cheese (60g)); whole wheat pita bread (1 pita, 60g)

Instructions:

1. Marinate pork cubes in olive oil, lemon juice, garlic, oregano, salt, and pepper for at least 1 hour.
2. Thread pork onto skewers. Grill over medium heat until cooked through, about 5 minutes per side.
3. Prepare Greek salad by mixing tomatoes, cucumbers, olives, and feta. Dress with olive oil and lemon juice.
4. Serve pork souvlaki with a side of tzatziki, Greek salad, and whole wheat pita bread.

Nutritional Facts (Per Serving): Calories: 500 | Sugars: 6g | Fat: 22g | Carbohydrates: 40g | Protein: 40g | Fiber: 5g | Sodium: 400mg

Chicken Cacciatore with Olives and Capers

Prep: 15 minutes | Cook: 45 minutes | Serves: 4

Ingredients:

- 4 chicken thighs (800g)
- 1 cup olives (150g), pitted
- 2 Tbsp capers (30g)
- 1 can diced tomatoes (14 oz or 400g)
- 1 onion (70g), sliced
- 2 cloves garlic, minced
- 2 Tbsp olive oil (30ml)
- 1/2 cup chicken broth (120ml)
- 1 tsp dried oregano (1g)
- Salt and pepper to taste
- Garnish: Roasted Mediterranean vegetables (zucchini (200g) and bell peppers (200g))

Instructions:

1. Season chicken thighs with salt and pepper. In a large skillet, heat olive oil over medium heat and brown the chicken on both sides. Remove and set aside.
2. In the same skillet, add onion and garlic. Sauté until soft.
3. Add diced tomatoes, olives, capers, chicken broth, and oregano. Bring to a simmer.
4. Return chicken to the skillet, cover, and simmer for 30 minutes, until chicken is cooked through.
5. Meanwhile, roast zucchini and bell peppers seasoned with olive oil, salt, and pepper at 400°F (200°C) for 20 minutes.
6. Serve chicken cacciatore with roasted vegetables on the side.

Nutritional Facts (Per Serving): Calories: 500 | Sugars: 6g | Fat: 28g | Carbohydrates: 20g | Protein: 40g | Fiber: 5g | Sodium: 800mg

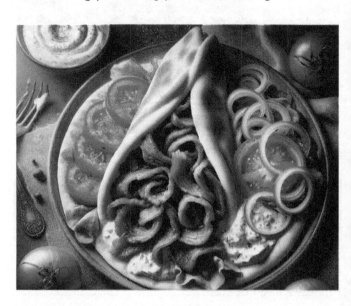

Gyros

Prep: 20 minutes | Cook: 20 minutes | Serves: 4

Ingredients:

- 1 lb seasoned gyro meat, thinly sliced (450g)
- 4 pita breads
- 1 cup tzatziki sauce (240g)
- 1 tomato, sliced (150g)
- 1 onion, thinly sliced (100g)

Instructions:

1. Cook gyro meat in a skillet over medium heat until crispy, about 3-5 minutes per side.
2. Warm pita breads in the oven or on the grill.
3. Assemble gyros with meat, tzatziki, tomato, and onion in pita breads.
4. Serve immediately.

Nutritional Facts (Per Serving): Calories: 500 | Sugars: 5g | Fat: 25g | Carbohydrates: 40g | Protein: 35g | Fiber: 3g | Sodium: 800mg

Grilled Skirt Steak with Chimichurri Sauce

Prep: 20 minutes (plus marinating) | Cook: 10 minutes | Serves: 4

Ingredients:

- 2 lbs skirt steak (900g)
- **For the Chimichurri Sauce:**
- 1/2 cup parsley (30g), finely chopped
- 1/4 cup olive oil (60ml)
- 2 Tbsp red wine vinegar (30ml)
- 3 cloves garlic, minced
- 1 tsp red pepper flakes (2g)
- Salt and pepper to taste
- Garnish: Quinoa tabbouleh made with 1 cup cooked quinoa (185g), 1/2 cup chopped parsley (15g), 1 cup diced tomatoes (180g), juice of 1 lemon

Instructions:

1. For the chimichurri, mix parsley, olive oil, red wine vinegar, garlic, red pepper flakes, salt, and pepper. Set aside.
2. Season skirt steak with salt and pepper. Grill over high heat to desired doneness, about 3-5 minutes per side for medium-rare.
3. Let steak rest for 5 minutes, then slice against the grain.
4. Serve steak topped with chimichurri sauce and a side of quinoa tabbouleh.

Nutritional Facts (Per Serving): Calories: 500 | Sugars: 3g | Fat: 25g | Carbohydrates: 20g | Protein: 50g | Fiber: 3g | Sodium: 200mg

Pork Tenderloin with Fig and Balsamic Reduction

Prep: 15 minutes | Cook: 25 minutes | Serves: 4

Ingredients:

- 1 lb pork tenderloin (450g)
- 1 cup figs (140g), quartered
- 1/2 cup balsamic vinegar (120ml)
- 2 Tbsp olive oil (30ml)
- Salt and pepper to taste
- Garnish: Grilled eggplant slices (200g) and arugula salad (100g) with vinaigrette (2 Tbsp olive oil, 1 Tbsp vinegar)

Instructions:

1. Preheat oven to 375°F (190°C). Season pork with salt and pepper.
2. Heat olive oil in a skillet over medium-high heat.
3. Sear pork on all sides.
4. Transfer pork to oven and roast for 15 minutes.
5. In the same skillet, add figs and balsamic vinegar. Cook until reduced by half.
6. Slice pork and serve with fig balsamic reduction, grilled eggplant, and arugula salad.

Nutritional Facts (Per Serving): Calories: 500 | Sugars: 12g | Fat: 20g | Carbohydrates: 30g | Protein: 40g | Fiber: 5g | Sodium: 200mg

Braised Beef with Mediterranean Herbs and Tomatoes

Prep: 20 minutes | Cook: 2 hours | Serves: 4

Ingredients:

- 1 lb beef chuck (450g)
- 1 can diced tomatoes (14.5 oz) (411g)
- 1/4 cup olive oil (60ml) (60g)
- 1 onion, chopped (110g)
- 2 cloves garlic, minced (10g)
- 1/2 cup beef broth (120ml) (120g)
- 2 tsp Mediterranean herb mix (thyme, rosemary, oregano) (2g)
- 2 cups green beans, trimmed (250g)
- 1 cup mashed sweet potatoes (200g)

Instructions:

1. Brown beef in olive oil, add onions and garlic, cook until soft.
2. Add tomatoes, broth, herbs, salt, and pepper. Simmer until beef is tender, about 2 hours.
3. Steam green beans until tender.
4. Serve beef with green beans and mashed sweet potatoes.

Nutritional Facts (Per Serving): Calories: 500 | Sugars: 10g | Fat: 25g | Carbohydrates: 30g | Protein: 35g | Fiber: 6g | Sodium: 80mg

Turkey and Spinach Meatballs in Lemon Broth

Prep: 20 minutes | Cook: 30 minutes | Serves: 4

Ingredients:

- 1 lb ground turkey (450g)
- 2 cups fresh spinach, chopped (60g)
- 1/4 cup breadcrumbs (30g)
- 1 egg, beaten
- 1 tsp salt (5g)
- 1/2 tsp black pepper (1g)
- 4 cups chicken broth (960ml) (960g)
- Juice and zest of 1 lemon
- 1 cup orzo pasta (200g)
- 1 Tbsp olive oil (15ml) (14g)
- 1/4 cup fresh parsley, chopped (15g)

Instructions:

1. Mix turkey, spinach, breadcrumbs, egg, salt, and pepper. Form into meatballs.
2. In a pot, bring chicken broth to a simmer, add lemon juice and zest.
3. Add meatballs to the broth and simmer until cooked through, about 20 minutes.
4. Cook orzo pasta according to package instructions, toss with olive oil and parsley.
5. Serve meatballs in lemon broth with a side of orzo.

Nutritional Facts (Per Serving): Calories: 500 | Sugars: 3g | Fat: 15g | Carbohydrates: 50g | Protein: 35g | Fiber: 3g | Sodium: 800mg

Chicken Parmesan (Parmigiana)

Prep: 15 minutes | Cook: 30 minutes | Serves: 4

Ingredients:

- 4 chicken breasts, pounded thin (6 oz each, 170g each)
- 1 cup breadcrumbs (120g)
- 1/2 cup grated Parmesan cheese (50g)
- 1 cup marinara sauce (240 ml)
- 1 cup shredded mozzarella cheese (100g)
- 2 tbsp olive oil (30 ml)
- Salt and pepper to taste

Instructions:

1. Season chicken with salt and pepper. Mix breadcrumbs and Parmesan, coat chicken.
2. Heat olive oil in a skillet, cook chicken until golden, about 4 minutes per side.
3. Place chicken in a baking dish, top with marinara and mozzarella.
4. Bake at 375°F (190°C) for 20 minutes until cheese is bubbly.

Nutritional Facts (Per Serving): Calories: 500 | Sugars: 5g | Fat: 20g | Carbohydrates: 30g | Protein: 50g | Fiber: 2g | Sodium: 900mg

Moussaka

Prep: 30 minutes | Cook: 1 hour | Serves: 6

Ingredients:

- 1 lb ground lamb (450g)
- 2 eggplants, sliced (600g)
- 2 potatoes, sliced (300g)
- 1 onion, chopped (150g)
- 2 cloves garlic, minced
- 1 can crushed tomatoes (14 oz, 400g)
- 1/4 cup all-purpose flour (30g)
- 2 cups milk (475 ml)
- 1/4 tsp ground cinnamon (1.25 ml)
- 1/4 tsp ground nutmeg (1.25 ml)
- 1/2 cup grated Parmesan cheese (50g)
- 3 tbsp olive oil (45 ml)
- Salt and pepper to taste

Instructions:

1. Fry eggplant and potato slices in olive oil until golden. Set aside on paper towels.
2. Sauté onion and garlic, add lamb, brown. Stir in tomatoes, cinnamon, and nut, simmer.
3. Arrange a layer of potatoes in a baking dish, top with meat sauce, then eggplant.
4. Make béchamel sauce: cook flour in butter, whisk in milk until thickened, stir in cheese.
5. Pour sauce over eggplant, bake at 350°F (175°C) for 45 minutes until golden.
6. Let rest before serving.

Nutritional Facts (Per Serving): Calories: 500 | Sugars: 8g | Fat: 30g | Carbohydrates: 35g | Protein: 25g | Fiber: 5g | Sodium: 600mg

CHAPTER 11: SNACK
Reinventing Snacking: Nutritious and Satisfying Bites

Olive Tapenade on Whole Grain Crackers

Prep: 10 minutes | Cook: 0 minutes | Serves: 4

Ingredients:

- 1 cup pitted kalamata olives (150g)
- 2 tbsp capers (25g)
- 1 clove garlic, minced
- 2 tbsp olive oil (30ml)
- 1 tbsp lemon juice (15ml)
- 1/4 tsp black pepper (1g)
- 16 whole grain crackers (100g)

Instructions:

1. Blend olives, capers, garlic, olive oil, lemon juice, and black pepper until smooth.
2. Spread the tapenade evenly over the crackers.

Nutritional Facts (Per Serving): Calories: 220 | Sugars: 2g | Fat: 18g | Carbohydrates: 16g | Protein: 3g | Fiber: 3g | Sodium: 580mg

Mini Bell Peppers Stuffed with Feta and Dill

Prep: 15 minutes | Cook: 10 minutes | Serves: 4

Ingredients:

- 12 mini bell peppers, halved and seeded (300g)
- 1 cup feta cheese, crumbled (150g)
- 2 tbsp fresh dill, chopped (6g)
- 1 tbsp olive oil (15ml)
- 1/4 tsp black pepper (1g)

Instructions:

1. Preheat oven to 375°F (190°C).
2. Mix feta, dill, olive oil, and black pepper in a bowl.
3. Stuff each bell pepper half with the feta mixture.
4. Bake for 10 minutes or until peppers are tender.

Nutritional Facts (Per Serving): Calories: 220 | Sugars: 5g | Fat: 16g | Carbohydrates: 12g | Protein: 7g | Fiber: 2g | Sodium: 420mg

Avocado and Lime Guacamole with Baked Pita Chips

Prep: 15 minutes | Cook: 10 minutes | Serves: 4

Ingredients:

- 2 avocados, mashed (300g)
- Juice and zest of 1 lime
- 1/4 cup red onion, finely chopped (40g)
- 1/4 tsp salt (1g)
- 1/4 tsp black pepper (1g)
- 4 whole wheat pita breads, cut into 8 wedges each (200g)
- 1 tbsp olive oil (15ml)

Instructions:

1. Preheat oven to 350°F (180°C).
2. Toss pita wedges with olive oil and spread on a baking sheet.
3. Bake for 10 minutes or until crispy.
4. Mix mashed avocado, lime juice and zest, red onion, salt, and pepper in a bowl.
5. Serve guacamole with baked pita chips.

Nutritional Facts (Per Serving): Calories: 220 | Sugars: 3g | Fat: 14g | Carbohydrates: 23g | Protein: 4g | Fiber: 7g | Sodium: 300mg

Rosemary and Grape Focaccia Bites

Prep: 20 minutes | Cook: 20 minutes | Serves: 8

Ingredients:

- 1/2 lb fresh pizza dough (225g)
- 1 tbsp olive oil (15ml)
- 1/2 cup red grapes, halved (75g)
- 1 tbsp fresh rosemary, chopped (1.5g)
- 1/4 tsp sea salt (1.5g)
- 1/4 tsp black pepper (1g)

Instructions:

1. Preheat oven to 450°F (230°C).
2. Roll out pizza dough on a baking sheet and brush with olive oil.
3. Top with halved grapes and sprinkle with rosemary, salt, and pepper.
4. Bake for 20 minutes or until the crust is golden and crisp.
Cut into bite-sized pieces before serving.

Nutritional Facts (Per Serving): Calories: 220 | Sugars: 5g | Fat: 5g | Carbohydrates: 38g | Protein: 5g | Fiber: 2g | Sodium: 290mg

CHAPTER 12: DESSERTS
Energy-Boosting Desserts: Perfect for Midday Slumps

Oat and Nut Protein Bars

Prep: 15 minutes | Cook: 0 minutes | Serves: 8

Ingredients:

- 1 cup rolled oats (90g)
- 1/2 cup mixed nuts, chopped (60g)
- 1/4 cup honey (60ml)
- 1/2 cup peanut butter (120g)
- 1 tsp vanilla extract (5ml)
- 1/4 tsp salt (1.5g)

Instructions:

1. Mix all ingredients in a bowl until well combined.
2. Press the mixture into a lined 8x8 inch (20x20 cm) baking dish.
3. Chill in the refrigerator for at least 1 hour.
4. Cut into bars and serve.

Nutritional Facts (Per Serving): Calories: 220 | Sugars: 12g | Fat: 12g | Carbohydrates: 24g | Protein: 6g | Fiber: 3g | Sodium: 150mg

Peanut Butter and Jelly Energy Bites

Prep: 15 minutes | Cook: 0 minutes | Serves: 10

Ingredients:

- 1 cup oats (90g)
- 1/2 cup peanut butter (120g)
- 1/4 cup flax seeds (30g)
- 1 tbsp honey (15ml)
- 1/4 cup jelly (60g)

Instructions:

1. Mix all ingredients in a bowl until well combined.
2. Roll the mixture into small balls, about 1 inch (2.5 cm) in diameter.
3. Chill in the refrigerator for at least 30 minutes.
4. Serve chilled.

Nutritional Facts (Per Serving): Calories: 220 | Sugars: 9g | Fat: 12g | Carbohydrates: 23g | Protein: 7g | Fiber: 3g | Sodium: 75mg

Raspberry Ricotta Mini Galettes

Prep: 20 minutes | Cook: 25 minutes | Serves: 8

Ingredients:

- 1 cup all-purpose flour (120g)
- 1/4 cup unsalted butter, chilled and cubed (60g)
- 2-3 Tbsp ice water (30-45ml)
- 1/2 cup ricotta cheese (125g)
- 1/4 cup fresh raspberries (31g)
- 2 Tbsp granulated sugar, divided (25g)
- 1 egg, beaten for egg wash (50g)
- Pinch of salt

Instructions:

1. In a food processor, pulse flour, 1 Tbsp sugar, and salt. Add butter and pulse until mixture resembles coarse crumbs. Gradually add ice water until dough forms.
2. Divide dough into 8 small balls. On a floured surface, roll each ball into a 4-inch round.
3. Spread ricotta on each round, leaving a border.
4. Top with raspberries. Sprinkle with remaining sugar.
5. Fold edges over, leaving the center exposed. Brush with egg wash.
6. Bake at 375°F (190°C) for 25 minutes, until golden.
Serve warm or at room temperature.

Nutritional Facts (Per Serving): Calories: 220 | Sugars: 4g | Fat: 12g | Carbohydrates: 22g | Protein: 6g | Fiber: 1g | Sodium: 45mg

Mixed Berry and Yogurt Parfait

Prep: 10 minutes | Cook: 0 minutes | Serves: 2

Ingredients:

- 1 cup plain Greek yogurt (245g)
- 1/2 cup granola (60g)
- 1/2 cup mixed berries (strawberries, blueberries, raspberries) (70g)
- 1 tbsp honey (15ml)

Instructions:

1. Layer half of the yogurt in two glasses.
2. Add a layer of granola followed by a layer of mixed berries.
3. Drizzle with honey.
4. Repeat the layers with the remaining ingredients.

Nutritional Facts (Per Serving): Calories: 220 | Sugars: 18g | Fat: 6g | Carbohydrates: 34g | Protein: 10g | Fiber: 4g | Sodium: 50mg

Date and Almond Energy Balls

Prep: 15 minutes | Cook: 0 minutes | Serves: 8

Ingredients:

- 1 cup dates, pitted (175g)
- 1/2 cup almonds (70g)
- 1/4 cup shredded coconut (20g)
- 1 tbsp chia seeds (10g)

Instructions:

1. Blend dates and almonds in a food processor until a sticky dough forms.
2. Stir in chia seeds.
3. Roll the mixture into small balls, about 1 inch (2.5 cm) in diameter.
4. Roll the balls in shredded coconut.
5. Chill in the refrigerator before serving.

Nutritional Facts (Per Serving): Calories: 220 | Sugars: 18g | Fat: 10g | Carbohydrates: 30g | Protein: 4g | Fiber: 5g | Sodium: 5mg

Date and Almond Mini Tarts

Prep: 15 minutes | Cook: 20 minutes | Serves: 8

Ingredients:

- 1 cup almond flour (96g)
- 1/4 cup unsalted butter, melted (60g)
- 1/4 cup dates, pitted and chopped (40g)
- 2 Tbsp honey (30ml)
- 1 egg (50g)
- 1/4 tsp vanilla extract (1.25ml)
- Pinch of salt

Instructions:

1. Preheat oven to 350°F (175°C).
2. In a bowl, mix almond flour, melted butter, honey, vanilla extract, and salt until combined.
3. Press mixture into 8 mini tart pans.
4. Top each with chopped dates.
5. Beat egg and brush over the top.
6. Bake for 20 minutes, until set and golden.
7. Let cool before serving.

Nutritional Facts (Per Serving): Calories: 220 | Sugars: 9g | Fat: 16g | Carbohydrates: 16g | Protein: 5g | Fiber: 2g | Sodium: 30mg

CHAPTER 13: DESSERTS
Sweet Temptations: Healthy Mediterranean Desserts

Almond and Orange Blossom Biscotti

Prep: 15 minutes | Cook: 40 minutes | Serves:10

Ingredients:

- 2 cups all-purpose flour (240g)
- 3/4 cup sugar (150g)
- 1 tsp baking powder (5g)
- 1/2 cup almonds, chopped (60g)
- 2 large eggs (100g)
- 1 tbsp orange blossom water (15ml)
- Zest of 1 orange
- 1/4 tsp salt (1.5g)

Instructions:

1. Preheat oven to 350°F (175°C).
2. Combine flour, sugar, baking powder, almonds, orange zest, and salt in a bowl.
3. Beat eggs with orange blossom water, then add to the dry ingredients, forming a dough.
4. Shape into a log on a lined baking sheet, bake for 25 minutes, slice, and bake for another 15 minutes.

Nutritional Facts (Per Serving): Calories: 220 | Sugars: 15g | Fat: 5g | Carbohydrates: 38g | Protein: 5g | Fiber: 2g | Sodium: 90mg

Mini Lemon and Olive Oil Cakes

Prep: 20 minutes | Cook: 25 minutes | Serves: 8

Ingredients:

- 1 cup all-purpose flour (120g)
- 2/3 cup sugar (133g)
- 1/3 cup olive oil (80ml)
- 2 large eggs (100g)
- 1 lemon, zested and juiced
- 1/2 tsp baking powder (2.5g)
- 1/4 tsp salt (1.5g)

Instructions:

1. Preheat oven to 350°F (175°C).
2. Whisk together flour, baking powder, salt, lemon zest, and juice.
3. In a separate bowl, combine sugar, olive oil, and eggs.
4. Mix wet and dry ingredients, pour into molds, and bake for 25 minutes.

Nutritional Facts (Per Serving): Calories: 220 | Sugars: 16g | Fat: 10g | Carbohydrates: 28g | Protein: 3g | Fiber: 0.5g | Sodium: 150mg

Ricotta and Fig Crostini with Honey Drizzle

Prep: 10 minutes | Cook: 5 minutes | Serves: 8

Ingredients:

- 1 baguette, sliced (200g)
- 1 cup ricotta cheese (250g)
- 8 figs, sliced (240g)
- 2 tbsp honey (30ml)
- 1/4 cup walnuts, chopped (30g)

Instructions:

1. Broil baguette slices until golden.
2. Spread ricotta on each slice, top with figs, drizzle with honey, and sprinkle with walnuts.

Nutritional Facts (Per Serving): Calories: 220 | Sugars: 15g | Fat: 8g | Carbohydrates: 29g | Protein: 8g | Fiber: 2g | Sodium: 200mg

Sesame and Honey Halva Squares

Prep: 10 minutes | Cook: 5 minutes | Serves: 10

Ingredients:

- 1 cup tahini (sesame paste) (240g)
- 1/2 cup honey (120ml)
- 1 tsp vanilla extract (5ml)
- 1/2 cup sesame seeds, toasted (70g)
- 1/4 tsp salt (1.5g)

Instructions:

1. Heat honey until it becomes slightly foamy.
2. Mix tahini, vanilla extract, and salt in a bowl.
3. Pour warm honey into the tahini mixture and stir in sesame seeds.
4. Press the mixture into a lined square dish and cool until set.
5. Cut into squares and serve.

Nutritional Facts (Per Serving): Calories: 220 | Sugars: 12g | Fat: 16g | Carbohydrates: 18g | Protein: 5g | Fiber: 2g | Sodium: 60mg

Mini Berry and Mascarpone Tarts

Prep: 20 minutes | Cook: 10 minutes | Serves: 8

Ingredients:

- 8 mini tart shells (160g)
- 1 cup mascarpone cheese (240g)
- 1/4 cup powdered sugar (30g)
- 1 tsp vanilla extract (5ml)
- 1 cup mixed berries (strawberries, blueberries, raspberries) (120g)

Instructions:

1. Bake tart shells as per package instructions and let cool.
2. Mix mascarpone, powdered sugar, and vanilla until smooth.
3. Fill each tart shell with the mascarpone mixture.
4. Top with mixed berries.
5. Serve chilled.

Nutritional Facts (Per Serving): Calories: 220 | Sugars: 10g | Fat: 15g | Carbohydrates: 18g | Protein: 4g | Fiber: 1g | Sodium: 45mg

Espresso Affogato with Vanilla Gelato

Prep: 5 minutes | Cook: 0 minutes | Serves: 4

Ingredients:

- 4 scoops vanilla gelato (240g)
- 4 shots espresso (240ml)

Instructions:

1. Place one scoop of gelato in each serving glass.
2. Pour one shot of hot espresso over each gelato scoop.
3. Serve immediately.

Nutritional Facts (Per Serving): Calories: 220 | Sugars: 22g | Fat: 10g | Carbohydrates: 28g | Protein: 4g | Fiber: 0g | Sodium: 70mg

Apricot and Walnut Phyllo Cups

Prep: 15 minutes | Cook: 15 minutes | Serves: 8

Ingredients:

- 8 phyllo dough sheets (160g)
- 1/2 cup chopped apricots (65g)
- 1/4 cup honey (60ml)
- 1/2 tsp cinnamon (1g)
- 2 tbsp melted butter (30ml)
- 1/2 cup chopped walnuts (60g)

Instructions:

1. Preheat oven to 350°F (175°C).
2. Brush each phyllo sheet with melted butter, stack them, and cut into squares to fit into muffin tins.
3. Press phyllo squares into muffin tins, creating cups.
5. Mix apricots, walnuts, honey, and cinnamon, then spoon into phyllo cups.
6. Bake for 15 minutes or until golden brown.
7. Serve warm or at room temperature.

Nutritional Facts (Per Serving): Calories: 220 | Sugars: 15g | Fat: 10g | Carbohydrates: 30g | Protein: 3g | Fiber: 2g | Sodium: 150mg

Pomegranate and Yogurt Mousse

Prep: 20 minutes | Cook: 0 minutes | Serves: 4

Ingredients:

- 1 cup Greek yogurt (240g)
- 1/2 cup pomegranate juice (120ml)
- 1/4 cup honey (60ml)
- 1 tsp gelatin (5g)
- 1/4 cup hot water (60ml)
- 1/2 cup pomegranate seeds (90g)

Instructions:

1. Dissolve gelatin in hot water and mix with pomegranate juice and honey.
2. Blend the pomegranate mixture with Greek yogurt until smooth.
3. Pour into serving dishes and chill until set, about 2 hours.
4. Top with pomegranate seeds before serving.

Nutritional Facts (Per Serving): Calories: 220 | Sugars: 25g | Fat: 3g | Carbohydrates: 40g | Protein: 10g | Fiber: 1g | Sodium: 35mg

Lemon Sorbet with Mint

Prep: 10 minutes | Cook: 2 hours (freezing time) | Serves: 4

Ingredients:

- 1 cup water (240ml)
- 3/4 cup sugar (150g)
- 3/4 cup lemon juice (180ml)
- 1 tbsp lemon zest (6g)
- 1/4 cup fresh mint leaves, chopped (6g)

Instructions:

1. Boil water and sugar until sugar dissolves. Remove from heat and cool.
2. Stir in lemon juice, zest, and mint leaves.
3. Pour into a shallow dish and freeze until solid, stirring occasionally.
4. Serve chilled.

Nutritional Facts (Per Serving): Calories: 220 | Sugars: 50g | Fat: 0g | Carbohydrates: 56g | Protein: 0g | Fiber: 1g | Sodium: 5mg

Cherry and Almond Clafoutis

Prep: 15 minutes | Cook: 45 minutes | Serves: 8

Ingredients:

- 1 lb cherries, pitted (450g)
- 3/4 cup all-purpose flour (90g)
- 1/2 cup sugar (100g)
- 1/4 cup almond meal (25g)
- 1 cup milk (240ml)
- 3 large eggs (150g)
- 1 tsp almond extract (5ml)
- 1 tbsp unsalted butter, melted (15ml)
- Powdered sugar for dusting

Instructions:

1. Preheat oven to 350°F (175°C).
2. Arrange cherries in a buttered baking dish.
3. Whisk together flour, sugar, almond meal, milk, eggs, almond extract, and melted butter.
4. Pour the batter over the cherries and bake for 45 minutes.
5. Dust with powdered sugar before serving.

Nutritional Facts (Per Serving): Calories: 220 | Sugars: 25g | Fat: 6g | Carbohydrates: 35g | Protein: 6g | Fiber: 2g | Sodium: 45mg

Figs Stuffed with Mascarpone and Honey

Prep: 10 minutes | Cook: 0 minutes | Serves: 6

Ingredients:

- 12 fresh figs (360g)
- 1 cup mascarpone cheese (240g)
- 2 tbsp honey (30ml)
- 2 tbsp chopped almonds (15g)

Instructions:

1. Cut a cross at the top of each fig, not cutting all the way through.
2. Mix mascarpone and honey, then spoon into figs.
3. Sprinkle with almonds and serve.

Nutritional Facts (Per Serving): Calories: 220 | Sugars: 18g | Fat: 14g | Carbohydrates: 20g | Protein: 4g | Fiber: 3g | Sodium: 35mg

Fig and Honey Cheesecake

Prep: 20 minutes | Cook: 1 hour | Serves: 12

Ingredients:

- 1 1/2 cups graham cracker crumbs (150g)
- 1/4 cup unsalted butter, melted (60ml)
- 2 cups cream cheese (450g)
- 1/2 cup honey (120ml)
- 4 large eggs (200g)
- 1 tsp vanilla extract (5ml)
- 1 cup fresh figs, sliced (150g)

Instructions:

1. Preheat oven to 325°F (160°C).
2. Mix graham cracker crumbs with melted butter and press into the bottom of a springform pan.
3. Beat cream cheese, honey, eggs, and vanilla until smooth.
4. Pour over the crust and top with sliced figs.
5. Bake for 1 hour, then cool and refrigerate before serving.

Nutritional Facts (Per Serving, if each cake is divided into 12 equal parts): Calories: 220 | Sugars: 20g | Fat: 14g | Carbohydrates: 18g | Protein: 5g | Fiber: 1g | Sodium: 180mg

Raspberry and Dark Chocolate Macaroons

Prep: 20 minutes | Cook: 15 minutes | Serves: 10

Ingredients:

- 2 cups shredded coconut (160g)
- 3/4 cup raspberries (110g)
- 1/3 cup honey (80ml)
- 1 tsp vanilla extract (5ml)
- 2 large egg whites (60g)
- 1/4 cup dark chocolate chips, melted (45g)

Instructions:

1. Preheat oven to 325°F (165°C).
2. Mash raspberries and mix with coconut, honey, vanilla, and egg whites.
3. Drop spoonfuls onto a baking sheet and bake for 15 minutes.
4. Drizzle with melted dark chocolate.
5. Cool before serving.

Nutritional Facts (Per Serving): Calories: 220 | Sugars: 18g | Fat: 14g | Carbohydrates: 24g | Protein: 3g | Fiber: 4g | Sodium: 45mg

Almond and Raspberry Clafoutis

Prep: 15 minutes | Cook: 40 minutes | Serves: 8

Ingredients:

- 1 cup raspberries (123g)
- 3/4 cup almond flour (75g)
- 1/2 cup granulated sugar (100g)
- 1 cup milk (240ml)
- 3 eggs (150g)
- 1 tsp almond extract (5ml)
- Powdered sugar for dusting

Instructions:

1. Preheat oven to 375°F (190°C).
2. Arrange raspberries in a greased baking dish.
3. Mix almond flour, sugar, milk, eggs, and almond extract; pour over raspberries.
4. Bake for 40 minutes and dust with powdered sugar.
5. Serve warm.

Nutritional Facts (Per Serving): Calories: 220 | Sugars: 20g | Fat: 12g | Carbohydrates: 20g | Protein: 6g | Fiber: 3g | Sodium: 70mg

Apricot and Pistachio Tartlets

Prep: 20 minutes | Cook: 25 minutes | Serves: 8

Ingredients:

- 1 cup all-purpose flour (120g)
- 1/2 cup butter, chilled (113g)
- 1/4 cup powdered sugar (30g)
- 1/2 cup apricot jam (140g)
- 1/4 cup pistachios, chopped (30g)
- 8 apricot halves (200g)

Instructions:

1. Preheat oven to 350°F (175°C).
2. Mix flour, butter, and powdered sugar to form dough. Press into tartlet pans.
3. Fill each with apricot jam, top with an apricot half and sprinkle with pistachios.
4. Bake for 25 minutes.
5. Cool before serving.

Nutritional Facts (Per Serving): Calories: 220 | Sugars: 15g | Fat: 12g | Carbohydrates: 26g | Protein: 3g | Fiber: 2g | Sodium: 70mg

Lemon Lavender Shortbread

Prep: 15 minutes | Cook: 20 minutes | Serves: 12

Ingredients:

- 1 cup all-purpose flour (120g)
- 1/3 cup granulated sugar (67g)
- 1/2 cup unsalted butter, softened (113g)
- 1 tbsp lemon zest (6g)
- 1 tsp dried lavender (1g)
- 1/4 tsp salt (1.5g)

Instructions:

1. Preheat oven to 350°F (175°C).
2. Mix flour, sugar, lemon zest, lavender, and salt.
3. Incorporate butter until the dough forms.
4. Press into a pan, bake for 20 minutes, then slice into squares.

Nutritional Facts (Per Serving): Calories: 220 | Sugars: 6g | Fat: 12g | Carbohydrates: 26g | Protein: 2g | Fiber: 0.5g | Sodium: 50mg

Orange and Almond Flourless Cake

Prep:15 minutes | Cook: 40 minutes | Serves: 8

Ingredients:

- 2 oranges (250g)
- 1 1/2 cups almond flour (150g)
- 1 cup granulated sugar (200g)
- 1 tsp baking powder (4g)
- 6 eggs (300g)

Instructions:

1. Boil oranges, blend into a puree.
2. Mix almond flour, sugar, baking powder, and eggs.
3. Fold in orange puree, bake in a greased pan at 375°F (190°C) for 40 minutes.

Nutritional Facts (Per Serving): Calories: 220 | Sugars: 22g | Fat: 12g | Carbohydrates: 24g | Protein: 6g | Fiber: 3g | Sodium: 125mg

Berry and Mascarpone Tart

Prep: 20 minutes | Cook: 20 minutes | Serves: 8

Ingredients:

- 1 prebaked tart shell (200g)
- 1 cup mascarpone cheese (240g)
- 1/4 cup powdered sugar (30g)
- 1 cup mixed berries (150g)
- 1 tbsp honey (15ml)

Instructions:

1. Mix mascarpone with powdered sugar.
2. Spread mixture in tart shell, top with berries.
3. Drizzle with honey, chill before serving.

Nutritional Facts (Per Serving): Calories: 220 | Sugars: 15g | Fat: 14g | Carbohydrates: 20g | Protein: 3g | Fiber: 2g | Sodium: 60mg

CHAPTER 14: DINNER
Light and Flavorful Evening Meals

Baked Trout with Almond and Parsley Crust, Served with Arugula Salad

Prep: 20 minutes | Cook: 15 minutes | Serves: 2

Ingredients:

- 2 trout fillets (200g each)
- 1/4 cup almonds, crushed (30g)
- 2 Tbsp parsley, finely chopped (8g)
- 1 Tbsp olive oil (15ml)
- 2 cups arugula (60g)
- 1/2 lemon, juice and zest
- Salt and pepper to taste

Instructions:

1. Preheat oven to 400°F (200°C). Season trout fillets with salt and pepper.
2. Mix crushed almonds, parsley, lemon zest, and a tablespoon of olive oil in a bowl. Press onto the top of each fillet.
3. Bake in the preheated oven until the crust is golden and fish flakes easily, about 15 minutes.
4. Toss arugula with lemon juice and remaining olive oil. Season with salt and pepper.
5. Serve baked trout over the arugula salad.

Nutritional Facts (Per Serving): Calories: 380 | Sugars: 2g | Fat: 22g | Carbohydrates: 6g | Protein: 38g | Fiber: 3g | Sodium: 120mg

Broccoli and Quinoa Salad with Honey Mustard Dressing

Prep: 15 minutes | Cook: 20 minutes | Serves: 2

Ingredients:

- 1 cup broccoli florets (90g)
- 1/2 cup quinoa, uncooked (85g)
- 2 Tbsp almonds, sliced (15g)
- 1 Tbsp mustard (15g)
- 1 Tbsp olive oil (15ml)
- 2 Tbsp lemon juice (30ml)
- Salt and pepper to taste
- 1 Tbsp honey (21g)

Instructions:

1. Cook quinoa according to package instructions; let cool.
2. Steam broccoli florets until tender-crisp, about 3-4 minutes; let cool.
3. In a small bowl, whisk together honey, mustard, olive oil, and lemon juice for the dressing.
4. Toss the cooled quinoa, broccoli, and sliced almonds with the dressing. Season with salt and pepper.
5. Serve chilled or at room temperature.

Nutritional Facts (Per Serving): Calories: 380 | Sugars: 9g | Fat: 15g | Carbohydrates: 53g | Protein: 12g | Fiber: 7g | Sodium: 200mg

Cajun-Spiced Shrimp and Cauliflower Grits

Prep: 10 minutes | Cook: 20 minutes | Serves: 2

Ingredients:

- 12 large shrimp, peeled and deveined (180g)
- 1 Tbsp Cajun seasoning (8g)
- 1 Tbsp olive oil (15ml)
- 2 cups cauliflower, riced (200g)
- 1 cup vegetable broth (240ml)
- 1/4 cup Parmesan cheese, grated (30g)
- Salt and pepper to taste

Instructions:

1. Toss shrimp with Cajun seasoning until evenly coated.
2. Heat olive oil in a skillet over medium heat. Add shrimp and cook until pink and opaque, about 2-3 minutes per side. Remove and set aside.
3. In the same skillet, add riced cauliflower and vegetable broth. Cook until tender and liquid is mostly absorbed, about 10 minutes.
4. Stir in Parmesan cheese until melted and season with salt and pepper.
5. Serve Cajun-spiced shrimp over cauliflower grits.

Nutritional Facts (Per Serving): Calories: 380 | Sugars: 5g | Fat: 18g | Carbohydrates: 18g | Protein: 38g | Fiber: 4g | Sodium: 650mg

Grilled Tuna Steak with Tomato and Olive Salsa, Served with a Fennel Salad

Prep: 15 minutes | Cook: 10 minutes | Serves: 2

Ingredients:

- 2 tuna steaks (150g each)
- 1 cup cherry tomatoes, halved (150g)
- 1/4 cup black olives, pitted and chopped (30g)
- 1 small red onion, finely chopped (70g)
- 1 Tbsp lemon juice (15ml)
- 1 fennel bulb, thinly sliced (200g)
- 1/4 cup fresh parsley, chopped (15g)
- Salt and pepper to taste
- 2 Tbsp olive oil (30ml)

Instructions:

1. Preheat grill to medium-high heat. Season tuna steaks with salt and pepper.
2. Grill tuna steaks for 4-5 minutes per side, or until desired doneness.
3. In a bowl, combine cherry tomatoes, black olives, red onion, 1 Tbsp olive oil, lemon juice, and parsley. Season with salt and pepper to make the salsa.
4. Toss sliced fennel with remaining olive oil and season with salt and pepper to make the salad.
5. Serve grilled tuna steaks topped with tomato and olive salsa, accompanied by the fennel salad.

Nutritional Facts (Per Serving): Calories: 380 | Sugars: 5g | Fat: 22g | Carbohydrates: 12g | Protein: 34g | Fiber: 3g | Sodium: 300mg

Spinach and Feta Stuffed Portobello Mushrooms

Prep: 15 minutes | Cook: 20 minutes | Serves: 2

Ingredients:

- 4 large Portobello mushroom caps (200g)
- 2 cups spinach, chopped (60g)
- 1/2 cup feta cheese, crumbled (75g)
- 1/4 cup red onions, finely diced (40g)
- 2 Tbsp olive oil (30ml)
- 2 cloves garlic, minced (6g)
- Salt and pepper to taste

Instructions:

1. Preheat oven to 375°F (190°C). Remove stems and gills from mushrooms.
2. Sauté spinach, garlic, and red onions in 1 Tbsp olive oil until spinach is wilted.
3. Remove from heat and stir in feta cheese. Season with salt and pepper.
4. Fill each mushroom cap with the spinach and feta mixture. Drizzle with remaining olive oil.
5. Bake for 20 minutes, or until mushrooms are tender and the filling is heated through.

Nutritional Facts (Per Serving): Calories: 380 | Sugars: 4g | Fat: 28g | Carbohydrates: 12g | Protein: 18g | Fiber: 3g | Sodium: 600mg

Zucchini Noodles with Pesto and Cherry Tomatoes

Prep: 10 minutes | Cook: 5 minutes | Serves: 2

Ingredients:

- 4 cups zucchini noodles (400g)
- 1/2 cup cherry tomatoes, halved (75g)
- 1/4 cup pesto sauce (60g)
- 2 Tbsp pine nuts, toasted (15g)
- 1/4 cup Parmesan cheese, grated (30g)
- Salt and pepper to taste

Instructions:

1. Heat a large skillet over medium heat. Add zucchini noodles, tossing until warmed, about 2-3 minutes.
2. Add cherry tomatoes and pesto sauce to the noodles. Toss until evenly coated.
3. Serve zucchini noodles topped with pine nuts and grated Parmesan cheese.
4. Season with salt and pepper to taste.

Nutritional Facts (Per Serving): Calories: 380 | Sugars: 6g | Fat: 30g | Carbohydrates: 14g | Protein: 12g | Fiber: 4g | Sodium: 480mg

Pan-Seared Tilapia with Lemon Caper Sauce and Green Beans

Prep: 10 minutes | Cook: 15 minutes | Serves: 2

Ingredients:

- 2 tilapia fillets (140g each)
- 2 Tbsp olive oil (30ml)
- 1/4 cup capers, drained (30g)
- Juice of 1 lemon (45ml)
- 1/2 cup chicken broth (120ml)
- 2 cups green beans, trimmed (200g)
- Salt and pepper to taste

Instructions:

1. eason tilapia fillets with salt and pepper.
2. Heat 1 Tbsp olive oil in a skillet over medium heat. Add tilapia and cook until golden brown, about 3-4 minutes per side. Remove and set aside.
3. In the same skillet, add lemon juice, chicken broth, and capers. Simmer until the sauce is reduced by half.
4. In another skillet, heat the remaining olive oil. Add green beans and sauté until tender-crisp, about 5 minutes. Season with salt and pepper.
5. Serve the tilapia topped with lemon caper sauce, alongside green beans.

Nutritional Facts (Per Serving): Calories: 380 | Sugars: 4g | Fat: 22g | Carbohydrates: 12g | Protein: 34g | Fiber: 4g | Sodium: 520mg

Grilled Sardines with Olive Tapenade and Mixed Greens

Prep: 15 minutes | Cook: 10 minutes | Serves: 2

Ingredients:

- 8 fresh sardines, cleaned and gutted (400g)
- 2 Tbsp olive tapenade (30g)
- 1 Tbsp olive oil (15ml)
- Juice of 1/2 lemon (22ml)
- Salt and pepper to taste
- 4 cups mixed greens (120g)

Instructions:

1. Preheat grill to medium-high. Season sardines with salt and pepper.
2. Grill sardines for 2-3 minutes per side, or until cooked through.
3. Toss mixed greens with olive oil, lemon juice, and a pinch of salt and pepper.
4. Serve grilled sardines with a dollop of olive talented and a side of mixed greens.

Nutritional Facts (Per Serving): Calories: 380 | Sugars: 2g | Fat: 26g | Carbohydrates: 4g | Protein: 32g | Fiber: 2g | Sodium: 610mg

Grilled Zucchini and Bell Pepper with Feta

Prep: 10 minutes | Cook: 15 minutes | Serves: 2

Ingredients:

- 2 zucchinis, sliced lengthwise (400g)
- 1 red bell pepper, sliced (150g)
- 2 Tbsp olive oil (30ml)
- 1/2 cup feta cheese, crumbled (75g)
- 1 Tbsp fresh basil, chopped (2.5g)
- Salt and pepper to taste

Instructions:

1. Preheat grill to medium heat. Toss zucchini and bell pepper slices with 1 Tbsp olive oil, salt, and pepper.
2. Grill vegetables until tender and slightly charred, about 3-4 minutes per side.
3. Arrange grilled vegetables on a plate. Sprinkle with feta cheese and fresh basil.
4. Drizzle with remaining olive oil before serving.

Nutritional Facts (Per Serving): Calories: 380 | Sugars: 7g | Fat: 29g | Carbohydrates: 14g | Protein: 12g | Fiber: 4g | Sodium: 520mg

Cauliflower Steaks with Tahini Drizzle

Prep: 10 minutes | Cook: 20 minutes | Serves: 2

Ingredients:

- 1 large cauliflower, sliced into 1/2 inch thick steaks (500g total)
- 2 Tbsp olive oil (30ml)
- 2 Tbsp tahini (30g)
- 1 Tbsp lemon juice (15ml)
- 1 clove garlic, minced (3g)
- 1/4 tsp smoked paprika (1g)
- Salt and pepper to taste
- 1 Tbsp parsley, chopped for garnish (3.8g)

Instructions:

1. Preheat oven to 425°F (220°C). Line a baking sheet with parchment paper.
2. Brush both sides of cauliflower steaks with olive oil and season with salt and pepper.
3. Place cauliflower steaks on the prepared baking sheet and roast until tender and golden, about 20 minutes, flipping halfway through.
4. In a small bowl, whisk together tahini, lemon juice, minced garlic, smoked paprika, and a pinch of salt until smooth. If the sauce is too thick, add water a teaspoon at a time until desired consistency is reached.
5. Drizzle tahini sauce over roasted cauliflower steaks and garnish with chopped parsley.
6. Serve immediately.

Nutritional Facts (Per Serving): Calories: 380 | Sugars: 5g | Fat: 28g | Carbohydrates: 29g | Protein: 9g | Fiber: 6g | Sodium: 200mg

Falafel with Tahina and Fresh Vegetables

Prep: 20 minutes | Cook: 10 minutes | Serves: 4

Ingredients:

- 2 cups dried chickpeas (400g), soaked overnight
- 1/4 cup parsley (15g), chopped
- 1/4 cup cilantro (15g), chopped
- 1 small onion (70g), chopped
- 2 cloves garlic, minced
- 1 tsp cumin (2g)
- 1 tsp coriander (2g)
- Salt and pepper to taste
- Oil for frying
- For serving: tahina sauce, diced tomatoes (150g), sliced cucumbers (100g), and lettuce leaves (50g)
- 4 Tbsp tahina (60ml)
- Juice of 1 lemon

Instructions:

1. In a food processor, combine soaked chickpeas, parsley, cilantro, onion, garlic, cumin, coriander, salt, and pepper. Pulse until mixture is finely ground.
2. Form the mixture into small balls or patties.
3. Heat oil in a deep fryer or large pan to 375°F (190°C). Fry falafel in batches until golden, about 4-5 minutes.

4. Serve falafel with tahina sauce (mix tahina with lemon juice and a little water to thin), fresh vegetables, and lettuce wraps.

Nutritional Facts (Per Serving): Calories: 380 | Sugars: 6g | Fat: 22g | Carbohydrates: 60g | Protein: 18g | Fiber: 12g | Sodium: 300mg

Stewed Artichokes with Lemon

Prep: 15 minutes | Cook: 25 minutes | Serves: 4

Ingredients:

- 8 artichoke hearts (400g), quartered
- 2 cloves garlic, minced
- Juice and zest of 1 lemon
- 2 Tbsp olive oil (30ml)
- 1 cup vegetable broth (240ml)
- 1 tsp dried oregano (1g)
- Salt and pepper to taste

Instructions:

1. In a large pan, heat olive oil over medium heat.
2. Add garlic and cook until fragrant.
3. Add artichoke hearts, lemon juice, lemon zest, vegetable broth, oregano, salt, and pepper.
4. Bring to a simmer, cover, and cook for about 20 minutes, or until artichokes are tender.
5. Adjust seasoning to taste. Serve hot.

Nutritional Facts (Per Serving): Calories: 380 | Sugars: 3g | Fat: 14g | Carbohydrates: 80g | Protein: 15g | Fiber: 15g | Sodium: 300mg

CHAPTER 15: DINNER
Salad Feasts: A Symphony of Freshness and Taste

Provencal Nicoise Salad

Prep: 20 minutes | Cook: 10 minutes | Serves: 2

Ingredients:

- 2 eggs (100g)
- 4 oz green beans, trimmed (115g)
- 1 can tuna in olive oil, drained (140g)
- 1/2 cup cherry tomatoes, halved (100g)
- 1/4 cup small black olives (30g)
- 2 Tbsp extra virgin olive oil (30ml)
- 1 Tbsp red wine vinegar (15ml)
- 1 tsp Dijon mustard (5g)
- Salt and pepper to taste
- 2 cups mixed salad greens (50g)
- 4 small new potatoes, boiled and quartered (200g)

Instructions:

1. Boil eggs for 7 minutes for semi-soft yolks, cool in ice water, then peel and halve.

2. Blanch green beans in boiling water for 3 minutes, then cool in ice water.

3. Arrange salad greens on plates. Top with tuna, potatoes, green beans, tomatoes, olives, and eggs.

4. Whisk together olive oil, vinegar, mustard, salt, and pepper to make the dressing. Drizzle over the salad.

5. Serve immediately.

Nutritional Facts (Per Serving): Calories: 380 | Sugars: 4g | Fat: 22g | Carbohydrates: 24g | Protein: 24g | Fiber: 5g | Sodium: 580mg

Tabbouleh with Couscous and Numerous Herbs

Prep: 15 minutes | Cook: 5 minutes | Serves: 4

Ingredients:

- 1 cup couscous (200g)
- 2 cups parsley, finely chopped (60g)
- 1 cup mint, finely chopped (30g)
- 2 tomatoes, finely diced (200g)
- 1 cucumber, finely diced (150g)
- Juice of 2 lemons
- 3 Tbsp olive oil (45ml)
- Salt and pepper to taste
-

Instructions:

1. Prepare couscous according to package instructions. Fluff with a fork and let cool.

2. In a large bowl, combine parsley, mint, tomatoes, cucumber, lemon juice, olive oil, salt, and pepper.

3. Add cooled couscous to the bowl. Mix well.

4. Chill in the refrigerator for at least 1 hour before serving to allow flavors to meld.

Nutritional Facts (Per Serving): Calories: 380 | Sugars: 5g | Fat: 15g | Carbohydrates: 75g | Protein: 15g | Fiber: 8g | Sodium: 300mg

Mediterranean Chickpea Salad with Herbs and Feta

Prep: 15 minutes | Cook: 0 minutes | Serves: 2

Ingredients:

- 1 can chickpeas, rinsed and drained (400g)
- 1/2 cup cherry tomatoes, halved (100g)
- 1/4 cup red onion, finely chopped (40g)
- 1/4 cup cucumber, diced (50g)
- 1/4 cup feta cheese, crumbled (50g)
- 2 Tbsp extra virgin olive oil (30ml)
- 1 Tbsp lemon juice (15ml)
- 1/4 cup fresh parsley, chopped (15g)
- 1/4 cup fresh mint, chopped (15g)
- Salt and pepper to taste

Instructions:

1. In a large bowl, combine chickpeas, tomatoes, onion, cucumber, and feta cheese.
2. In a small bowl, whisk together olive oil, lemon juice, salt, and pepper.
3. Pour dressing over the chickpea mixture and toss to coat.
4. Gently fold in parsley and mint.
5. Serve immediately or chill in the refrigerator before serving.

Nutritional Facts (Per Serving): Calories: 380 | Sugars: 6g | Fat: 22g | Carbohydrates: 36g | Protein: 14g | Fiber: 10g | Sodium: 320mg

Salad with Smoked Salmon, Avocado, and Green Salad

Prep: 10 minutes | Cook: 0 minutes | Serves: 2

Ingredients:

- 4 oz smoked salmon (113g)
- 1 avocado, sliced (200g)
- 4 cups mixed green salad (spinach, arugula, lettuce) (120g)
- 1 Tbsp olive oil (15ml)
- 2 tsp lemon juice (10ml)
- Salt and pepper to taste

Instructions:

1. Arrange mixed greens on plates.
2. Top with slices of smoked salmon and avocado.
3. Drizzle with olive oil and lemon juice. Season with salt and pepper.
4. Serve immediately.

Nutritional Facts (Per Serving): Calories: 380 | Sugars: 2g | Fat: 28g | Carbohydrates: 12g | Protein: 22g | Fiber: 7g | Sodium: 600mg

Shrimp and Avocado Salad with Citrus Vinaigrette

Prep: 15 minutes | Cook: 5 minutes | Serves: 2

Ingredients:

- 8 oz shrimp, peeled and deveined (225g)
- 1 avocado, diced (200g)
- 4 cups mixed greens (120g)
- Juice of 1 orange (60ml)
- Juice of 1 lime (30ml)
- 1 tsp honey (5g)
- Salt and pepper to taste
- 2 Tbsp olive oil (30ml), divided

Instructions:

1. Heat 1 Tbsp olive oil in a pan over medium heat.
2. Add shrimp and cook until pink, about 2-3 minutes per side. Season with salt and pepper.
3. In a large bowl, mix the cooked shrimp, avocado, and mixed greens.
4. For the vinaigrette, whisk together the remaining olive oil, orange juice, lime juice, honey, salt, and pepper.
5. Dress the salad with the citrus vinaigrette and serve immediately.

Nutritional Facts (Per Serving): Calories: 380 | Sugars: 8g | Fat: 24g | Carbohydrates: 18g | Protein: 24g | Fiber: 7g | Sodium: 300mg

Fig, Prosciutto, and Arugula Salad

Prep: 10 minutes | Cook: 0 minutes | Serves: 2

Ingredients:

- 6 fresh figs, quartered (180g)
- 4 slices prosciutto (60g)
- 4 cups arugula (120g)
- 2 Tbsp olive oil (30ml)
- 1 Tbsp honey (15g)
- 1 Tbsp balsamic vinegar (15ml)
- Salt and pepper to taste

Instructions:

1. Arrange arugula on plates. Top with prosciutto and fig quarters.
2. In a small bowl, whisk together olive oil, honey, balsamic vinegar, salt, and pepper to make the dressing.
3. Drizzle the dressing over the salad before serving.

Nutritional Facts (Per Serving): Calories: 380 | Sugars: 24g | Fat: 18g | Carbohydrates: 46g | Protein: 10g | Fiber: 5g | Sodium: 320mg

Quinoa Salad with Roasted Vegetables

Prep: 15 minutes | Cook: 25 minutes | Serves: 2

Ingredients:

- 1/2 cup quinoa, uncooked (85g)
- 1 small zucchini, cubed (150g)
- 1 small bell pepper, cubed (150g)
- 1/2 red onion, chopped (100g)
- 2 Tbsp olive oil (30ml)
- 2 Tbsp lemon juice (30ml)
- 1/4 tsp salt (1.5g)
- 1/4 tsp black pepper (0.5g)
- 2 Tbsp fresh parsley, chopped (8g)

Instructions:

1. Preheat the oven to 400°F (200°C). Toss zucchini, bell pepper, and red onion with 1 Tbsp olive oil, salt, and pepper. Roast for 20 minutes, until tender.
2. Cook quinoa according to package instructions.
3. In a large bowl, combine roasted vegetables, cooked quinoa, remaining olive oil, lemon juice, and parsley. Toss well.
4. Serve at room temperature or chilled.

Nutritional Facts (Per Serving): Calories: 380 | Sugars: 5g | Fat: 14g | Carbohydrates: 56g | Protein: 10g | Fiber: 8g | Sodium: 300mg

Grilled Eggplant and Tomato Salad with Basil

Prep: 10 minutes | Cook: 10 minutes | Serves: 2

Ingredients:

- 1 large eggplant, sliced (300g)
- 2 tomatoes, sliced (200g)
- 2 Tbsp olive oil (30ml)
- 1 Tbsp balsamic vinegar (15ml)
- 1/4 cup fresh basil leaves, torn (6g)
- Salt and pepper to taste

Instructions:

1. Preheat grill to medium-high. Brush eggplant slices with 1 Tbsp olive oil and season with salt and pepper.
2. Grill eggplant for 3-4 minutes on each side, until tender.
3. Arrange eggplant and tomato slices on a plate. Drizzle with remaining olive oil and balsamic vinegar.
4. Garnish with fresh basil. Season with salt and pepper to taste.
5. Serve immediately.

Nutritional Facts (Per Serving): Calories: 380 | Sugars: 12g | Fat: 28g | Carbohydrates: 30g | Protein: 5g | Fiber: 9g | Sodium: 300mg

Pan-Fried Sole with Lemon Butter and Steamed Broccolini

Prep: 10 minutes | Cook: 15 minutes | Serves: 2

Ingredients:

- 2 sole fillets (150g each)
- 1 Tbsp unsalted butter (14g)
- Juice of 1/2 lemon (15ml)
- 1/2 lb broccolini, steamed (225g)
- Salt and pepper to taste

Instructions:

1. Season sole fillets with salt and pepper.
2. Heat butter in a pan over medium heat until melted. Add sole fillets and cook for 2-3 minutes on each side, until golden and cooked through.
3. Remove fillets from the pan, add lemon juice to the pan, and swirl to create the sauce.
4. Serve the sole drizzled with lemon butter and accompanied by steamed broccolini.

Nutritional Facts (Per Serving): Calories: 380 | Sugars: 2g | Fat: 18g | Carbohydrates: 6g | Protein: 48g | Fiber: 2g | Sodium: 200mg

Herb-Grilled Salmon with Lemon Quinoa

Prep: 15 minutes | Cook: 25 minutes | Serves: 2

Ingredients:

- 2 salmon fillets (150g each)
- 1/2 cup quinoa (90g)
- Juice and zest of 1 lemon (30ml juice)
- 1 Tbsp olive oil (15ml)
- 2 Tbsp fresh herbs (parsley, dill) chopped (8g)
- Salt and pepper to taste

Instructions:

1. Rinse quinoa under cold water. Cook quinoa according to package instructions, adding lemon zest and half of the lemon juice for flavor.
2. Season salmon with salt, pepper, and herbs. Drizzle with half the olive oil.
3. Grill salmon over medium heat for 4-5 minutes per side or until cooked through.
4. Fluff quinoa with a fork, stir in the remaining lemon juice and olive oil.
5. Serve the herb-grilled salmon over lemon quinoa.

Nutritional Facts (Per Serving): Calories: 380 | Sugars: 2g | Fat: 15g | Carbohydrates: 30g | Protein: 36g | Fiber: 4g | Sodium: 200mg

Shrimp and Feta Baked in Tomato Sauce, Served with Spinach

Prep: 10 minutes | Cook: 20 minutes | Serves: 2

Ingredients:

- 8 oz shrimp, peeled and deveined (225g)
- 1 cup tomato sauce (240ml)
- 1/2 cup feta cheese, crumbled (75g)
- 2 cups spinach (60g)
- 1 Tbsp olive oil (15ml)
- 1 garlic clove, minced (3g)
- Salt and pepper to taste

Instructions:

1. Preheat the oven to 375°F (190°C).
2. In a baking dish, combine shrimp, tomato sauce, and garlic. Season with salt and pepper.
3. Sprinkle feta cheese over the shrimp mixture.
4. Bake in the preheated oven for 15-20 minutes, until shrimp are pink and cooked through.
5. While the shrimp bakes, sauté spinach in olive oil until wilted, about 3-4 minutes.
6. Serve the shrimp and feta with the sautéed spinach on the side.

Nutritional Facts (Per Serving): Calories: 380 | Sugars: 6g | Fat: 20g | Carbohydrates: 12g | Protein: 38g | Fiber: 3g | Sodium: 800mg

Pan-Seared Halibut with Artichoke Hearts and Roasted Red Peppers

Prep: 10 minutes | Cook: 15 minutes | Serves: 2

Ingredients:

- 2 halibut fillets (6 oz each) (170g each)
- 1 cup artichoke hearts, quartered (140g)
- 1/2 cup roasted red peppers, sliced (100g)
- 2 Tbsp olive oil (30ml)
- 1 Tbsp lemon juice (15ml)
- Salt and pepper to taste
- 1 Tbsp fresh parsley, chopped (3.8g) for garnish

Instructions:

1. Season halibut fillets with salt and pepper.
2. Heat olive oil in a pan over medium heat. Add halibut and cook for 4-5 minutes on each side, until golden and cooked through.
3. In the same pan, add artichoke hearts and roasted red peppers. Sauté for 2-3 minutes, until heated through. Stir in lemon juice.
4. Serve halibut topped with artichoke and red pepper mixture, garnished with fresh parsley.

Nutritional Facts (Per Serving): Calories: 380 | Sugars: 2g | Fat: 22g | Carbohydrates: 8g | Protein: 38g | Fiber: 4g | Sodium: 300mg

Mussels in Garlic White Wine Sauce with a Side of Grilled Asparagus

Prep: 15 minutes | Cook: 15 minutes | Serves: 2

Ingredients:

- 1 lb mussels, cleaned and debearded (450g)
- 1 cup dry white wine (240ml)
- 2 cloves garlic, minced (6g)
- 2 Tbsp olive oil (30ml), divided
- 1/2 lb asparagus, ends trimmed (225g)
- Salt and pepper to taste
- 1 Tbsp parsley, chopped (3.8g) for garnish

Instructions:

1. In a large pot, heat 1 Tbsp olive oil over medium heat. Add garlic and sauté for 1 minute.
2. Add mussels and white wine. Cover and cook for 5-7 minutes, until mussels open. Discard any that do not open.
3. Meanwhile, brush asparagus with remaining olive oil, season with salt and pepper, and grill over medium heat for 4-5 minutes, until tender.
4. Serve mussels with their sauce, garnished with parsley, alongside grilled asparagus.

Nutritional Facts (Per Serving): Calories: 380 | Sugars: 2g | Fat: 22g | Carbohydrates: 14g | Protein: 24g | Fiber: 2g | Sodium: 500mg

Squid Stuffed with Herbed Couscous and Tomato Sauce

Prep: 20 minutes | Cook: 30 minutes | Serves: 2

Ingredients:

- 4 medium squid bodies, cleaned (200g)
- 1/2 cup couscous, cooked (90g)
- 1/4 cup tomato sauce (60ml)
- 1 Tbsp olive oil (15ml)
- 2 Tbsp fresh herbs (parsley, cilantro), chopped (8g)
- 1 clove garlic, minced (3g)
- Salt and pepper to taste

Instructions:

1. Preheat oven to 375°F (190°C).
2. Mix cooked couscous with herbs, half the garlic, salt, and pepper. Stuff this mixture into the squid bodies.
3. In a skillet, heat olive oil over medium heat. Add remaining garlic and sauté for 1 minute. Add tomato sauce and simmer for 5 minutes.
4. Place stuffed squid in a baking dish. Pour tomato sauce over squid.
5. Bake for 20 minutes, or until squid is tender.
6. Serve immediately.

Nutritional Facts (Per Serving): Calories: 380 | Sugars: 3g | Fat: 10g | Carbohydrates: 44g | Protein: 28g | Fiber: 2g | Sodium: 300mg

Baked Haddock with a Mediterranean Salsa Verde

Prep: 20 minutes | Cook: 15 minutes | Serves: 2

Ingredients:

- 2 haddock fillets (6 oz each, 170g)
- 2 Tbsp. olive oil (30 ml)
- 1 Tbsp. lemon juice (15 ml)

For Salsa Verde:
- 1/2 cup fresh parsley, chopped (15g)
- 1/4 cup fresh basil, chopped (15g)
- 1 Tbsp. capers, chopped (15g)
- 2 cloves garlic, minced (6g)
- 3 Tbsp. olive oil (45 ml)
- Salt and pepper to taste

Instructions:

1. Preheat oven to 400°F (200°C). Brush haddock with olive oil and lemon juice; season with salt and pepper.
2. Bake haddock for 12-15 minutes or until flaky.
3. Mix parsley, basil, capers, garlic, and olive oil for the salsa verde; season with salt and pepper.
4. Serve haddock topped with salsa verde.

Nutritional Facts (Per Serving): Calories: 380 | Sugars: 2g | Fat: 22g | Carbohydrates: 5g | Protein: 36g | Fiber: 1g | Sodium: 250mg

Crab Cakes with Remoulade and a Light Coleslaw

Prep: 30 minutes | Cook: 10 minutes | Serves: 2

Ingredients:

- 1/4 cup mayonnaise (60 ml)
- 1 Tbsp. capers, chopped (8g)
- 1 tsp. lemon juice (5 ml)

For Coleslaw:
- 1 cup shredded cabbage (70g)
- 1/4 cup shredded carrot (30g)
- 2 Tbsp. vinegar (30 ml)
- 1 tsp. honey (7 ml)

Instructions:

1. Mix crab meat, breadcrumbs, egg, mayonnaise, mustard, Worcestershire sauce, celery, parsley, salt, and pepper. Form into cakes.
2. Cook crab cakes in a skillet over medium heat until golden, about 5 minutes per side.
3. Mix mayonnaise, capers, and lemon juice for remoulade.
4. Toss cabbage and carrot with vinegar and honey for coleslaw.
5. Serve crab cakes with remoulade and coleslaw.

Nutritional Facts (Per Serving): Calories: 380 | Sugars: 5g | Fat: 20g | Carbohydrates: 20g | Protein: 25g | Fiber: 3g | Sodium: 700mg

CHAPTER 17: BONUSES

Meal Plans and Shopping Templates: The Key to Organized Meal Preparation

For a seamless integration of the Mediterranean diet into your daily routine, we've created a meticulously curated 30-day shopping blueprint that aligns with our cookbook's recipes. This tool is crafted to streamline your meal preparation process, prioritizing fresh and organic ingredients while steering clear of overly processed items. Keep an eye out for concealed sugars, particularly in condiments and salad dressings. Feel free to modify the suggested quantities to suit your personal dietary requirements, all while maintaining the Mediterranean focus on wholesome, unrefined foods. Delight in the art of healthful, tasteful cooking!

Grocery Shopping List for 7-Day Meal Plan

Proteins

Eggs (for omelettes and frittatas)
Feta cheese (for omelettes, salads, and bakes)
Trout (for Baked Trout with Almond and Parsley Crust)
Chicken breast (for Herbed Chicken and Vegetable Skillet)
Tuna steaks (for Grilled Tuna Steak with Tomato Olive Salsa)
Lamb (for Hearty Provencal Lamb Stew)
Sardines (for Grilled Sardines with Olive Tapenade)

Dairy and Dairy Alternatives:

Mozzarella cheese (for Caprese Salad)
Ricotta cheese (for bakes and quiches)
Mascarpone cheese (for Mini Berry and Mascarpone Tarts and Fig and Honey Cheesecake)
Parmesan cheese (for various dishes)

Fruits:

Tomatoes (for salads, gazpacho, and salsa)
Avocados (for guacamole)
Lemons (for zest and seasoning in various dishes)
Berries (for Mini Berry and Mascarpone Tarts and galettes)

Vegetables & Herbs:

Spinach (for omelettes, quiches, and bakes)
Eggplant, Zucchini (for frittatas and lasagna)
Asparagus (for risotto)
Garlic, onions, bell peppers (for stews, skillets, and sautés)
Fresh herbs like basil, parsley, thyme, and herbes de Provence (for flavoring and garnish)
Cucumbers (for gazpacho)

Grains & Bakery:

Whole grain crackers (for serving with tapenade)
Polenta (for Garlic Mushroom and Herb Polenta)
Farfalle and other pasta (for lasagna and Pasta Puttanesca)

Nuts & Seeds:

Almonds (for Andalusian Gazpacho and other recipes)
Pine nuts (for pesto in Farfalle with Spinach Pesto)

Pantry Staples:

Olive oil (for cooking and dressings)
Capers, olives (for Pasta Puttanesca and omelettes)
Vegetable broth (for soups and risotto)
Canned tomatoes, tomato paste (for soups, stews, and lasagna)
Pesto (for Provencal Vegetable Soup and other dishes)
Various spices (salt, pepper, red pepper flakes, etc.)

Miscellaneous:

Pita chips (for serving with guacamole)
Honey (for Fig and Honey Cheesecake)
Cocoa powder, dark chocolate (for desserts if needed)

Grocery Shopping List for 8-14 Day Meal Plan

Proteins

Feta cheese (for salads and yogurt bowl)
Ground meat (for Moussaka)
Eggs (for scrambles and breakfast bakes)
Lentils (for Lentil Soup)
Tortellini (preferably with spinach filling)
Halloumi cheese (for breakfast salad)
Various seafood (for Paella, including shrimp, mussels, clams)
Turkey (for breakfast meatballs)
Shrimp (for dinner on Day 14)

Dairy and Dairy Alternatives:

Greek yogurt (for yogurt bowl and parfait)
Ricotta cheese (for pancakes and crostini)
Mozzarella cheese (for risotto and pizza)
Parmesan cheese (for breakfast bake and salads)

Fruits:

Cucumbers (for yogurt bowl)

Mixed berries (for parfait)
Cherries (for clafoutis)
Lemons (for artichokes and other recipes)
Figs (for crostini)
Oranges (for biscotti)

Vegetables & Herbs:

Artichokes (for stew and breakfast bake)
Cherry tomatoes (for scramble and salads)
Various vegetables (for Moussaka, like eggplant and potatoes)
Spinach (for tortellini, crepes, and salads)
Fresh herbs (basil, thyme, parsley for various dishes)
Bell peppers, onions (for salads and paella)

Grains & Bakery:

Whole grain bread or crackers (for serving with parfait and tapenade)
Couscous (for tabbouleh)
Flour (for pancakes and cakes)

Nuts & Seeds:

Almonds (for energy balls and other recipes)
Walnuts (for pesto)
Sesame seeds (for halva squares)

Pantry Staples:

Olive oil (for cooking and dressings)
Tomato sauce and canned tomatoes (for Moussaka, pizza, and shrimp dish)

Various spices (salt, pepper, herbes de Provence, etc.)
Vegetable and chicken stock (for soups and risotto)
Pasta (penne for one of the lunches)
Miscellaneous:

Dates (for energy balls)
Honey (for crostini and other dishes)
Baking ingredients (baking powder, vanilla extract, etc. for pancakes and cakes)
Quinoa (for salmon dinner)

Grocery Shopping List for 15-21 Day Meal Plan

Proteins:

Cottage cheese (for Peachy Cottage Cheese Delight)
Pork (for Italian Pork Ragu)
Smoked salmon (for bagel)
Lamb (for Moroccan Lamb Tagine)
Shrimp (for Cajun-Spiced Shrimp and Cauliflower Grits)
Tuna (for breakfast salad)
Chicken sausage (for skillet)
Tilapia fillets (for Pan-Seared Tilapia)

Dairy and Dairy Alternatives:

Cream cheese (for bagel)
Feta cheese (for Avocado Toast and salad)
Greek yogurt (for parfait and mousse)
Vanilla gelato (for Espresso Affogato)
Mascarpone cheese (for figs)

97

Fruits and Vegetables:

Peaches (for cottage cheese delight)
Avocados (for toast)
Artichokes (for Moroccan Tagine)
Eggplants (for risotto)
Broccoli (for salad)
Mixed berries (for parfait)
Pomegranate (for mousse)
Figs (for stuffed figs)
Lemons (for various recipes)
Cherry tomatoes, arugula (for salad)

Grains, Nuts, & Bakery:

Bagels (for smoked salmon and cream cheese bagel)
Porcini mushrooms (for ragu)
Phyllo pastry (for cups)
Quinoa (for salad)
Pasta (for Puttanesca and Carbonara)

Herbs, Spices & Pantry Staples:

Pesto (for vegetable soup)
Espresso (for affogato)
Honey (for figs and dressing)
Peanut butter, jelly (for energy bites)
Capers, olives, anchovies (for Pasta Puttanesca)
Parmesan cheese, eggs, pancetta or guanciale (for Carbonara)

Miscellaneous:

Almonds (for trout crust and other dishes)
Olive oil, balsamic vinegar (for dressing and cooking)

Various spices (e.g., mint, Herbes de Provence, etc.)

Grocery Shopping List for 22-28 Day Meal Plan

Proteins:

Ground beef (for breakfast hash)
Chicken breasts (for Chicken Parmesan and pasta dish)
Turkey bacon (for muffins)
Sardines (for grilling)
Lamb (for stew)
Tortellini (preferably with spinach filling)
Mussels (for sauce)

Dairy and Dairy Alternatives:

Feta cheese (for mushrooms and salad)
Parmesan cheese (for Chicken Parmesan and risotto)
Mascarpone cheese (for cheesecake and tart)
Eggs (for breakfast dishes and muffins)
Milk (for oatmeal and other recipes)

Fruits and Vegetables:

Spinach (for hash, stuffed mushrooms, and salad)
Raspberries (for macaroons and clafoutis)
Zucchini, bell peppers (for grilling)
Pumpkins (for breakfast bowl)
Apricots, hazelnuts (for bulgur and tartlets)

Lemons (for cheesecake and shortbread)
Oranges (for flourless cake)
Asparagus (for grilling)

Grains, Nuts, & Bakery:

Barley (for breakfast bowl)
Oatmeal (for breakfast)
Bulgur (for breakfast bowl)
Almonds (for cake and tartlets)
Pistachios (for tartlets)
Hazelnuts (for bulgur)
Flourless (almond flour for cake)

Herbs, Spices & Pantry Staples:

Olive tapenade (for sardines)
Thyme, Herbes de Provence (for risotto and stew)
Garlic, onions (for various dishes)
Tomato sauce (for Penne Arrabbiata and Moussaka)
White wine (for mussels)
Dark chocolate (for macaroons)
Honey (for cheesecake)
Lavender (for shortbread)

Miscellaneous:

Bread crumbs (for Chicken Parmesan and Moussaka)
Artichokes (for pasta dish)
Fig (for cheesecake)
Raspberry jam (for macaroons)
Quinoa (for breakfast bowl)

Grocery Shopping List for 29-35 Day Meal Plan

Proteins:

Pork (for Souvlaki)
Turkey (for meatballs)
Shrimp (for salad)
Tilapia (for searing)
Beef (for braising)
Crab meat (for crab cakes)

Dairy and Dairy Alternatives:

Cottage cheese (for Peachy Cottage Cheese Delight)
Feta cheese (for stuffed peppers and orzo)
Halloumi cheese (for breakfast salad)
Greek yogurt (for Tzatziki)

Fruits and Vegetables:

Avocados (for creaminess and salad)
Pineapple (for creaminess)
Mini bell peppers (for stuffing)
Eggplant, zucchini (for frittata and salad)
Tomatoes, cucumber (for Gazpacho and Tabbouleh)
Raspberries (for oat fuel)
Mushrooms (for polenta)
Spinach (for meatballs)
Lemons (for various dishes)
Grapes (for focaccia)

Grains, Nuts, & Bakery:

Couscous (for Tabbouleh)
Oats (for oat fuel and protein bars)
Almonds (for Gazpacho and energy balls)
Whole grain crackers (for tapenade)
Pita (for guacamole)

Herbs, Spices & Pantry Staples:

Numerous fresh herbs (parsley, basil, dill, thyme, etc. for various dishes)
Polenta (for garlic mushroom dish)
Orzo (for grilled vegetable dish)
Olive oil, vinegar (for dressings and cooking)
Tapenade ingredients (olives, capers, anchovies)

Miscellaneous:

Espresso (for affogato)
Vanilla gelato (for affogato)
Dates (for energy balls)
Honey (for various recipes)
Crab cake ingredients (breadcrumbs, eggs, seasoning)

Grocery Shopping List for 36-42 Day Meal Plan

Proteins:

Chicken breast (for skillet)
Shrimp (for Cajun-spiced dish)
Ground beef (for Turkish stew)
Salmon (for smoked salmon bagel and baked trout)
Lamb (for stew)
Pork (for ragu)

Dairy and Dairy Alternatives:

Ricotta cheese (for bake)
Feta cheese (for yogurt bowl, scramble, and stuffed mushrooms)
Cream cheese (for bagel)
Parmesan cheese (for breakfast bake and pizza)

Fruits and Vegetables:

Cherry tomatoes (for penne and zucchini noodles)
Zucchini (for noodles)
Lemons (for pancakes and sorbet)
Eggplant (for Turkish stew)
Mixed berries (for parfait)
Broccoli (for salad)
Cucumbers (for yogurt bowl)
Arugula (for salad)
Apricots (for phyllo cups)

Grains, Nuts, & Bakery:

Penne pasta (for pesto penne)
Almonds (for penne and phyllo cups)
Whole grain or cauliflower grits (for Cajun dish)
Pizza dough (for Margherita)
Phyllo pastry (for cups)

Herbs, Spices & Pantry Staples:

Pesto (for penne and zucchini noodles)
Cajun seasoning (for shrimp dish)
Various fresh herbs (for skillet, stew, and soup)
Peanut butter, jelly (for energy bites)
Olive oil, vinegar (for dressings and cooking)
Honey (for parfait and dressing)
Espresso (for affogato)

Miscellaneous:

Vanilla gelato (for affogato)
Oats and nuts (for protein bars)
Walnuts (for phyllo cups)
Yogurt (for parfait and bowl)
Mint (for sorbet)

Grocery Shopping List for 43-49 Day Meal Plan

Proteins:

Mozzarella cheese (for Caprese salad)
Gorgonzola cheese (for risotto)
Salmon (for herb-grilled salmon)
Sardines (for grilling)
Chicken (for cacciatore)
Skirt steak (for grilling)
Halloumi cheese (for breakfast salad)

Dairy and Dairy Alternatives:

Ricotta cheese (for pancakes, bake, and lasagna)
Eggs (for frittata and quiche)
Yogurt (for parfait)

Fruits and Vegetables:

Tomatoes (for Caprese salad, cacciatore, and grilled salad)
Pumpkin (for risotto)
Raspberries (for galettes)
Spinach (for quiche, frittata, and crepes)
Eggplant, zucchini (for frittata and grilled salad)
Mixed berries (for parfait)
Avocado (for salad and guacamole)

Lemons (for salmon and quinoa)
Figs, arugula, prosciutto (for salad)

Grains, Nuts, & Bakery:

Quinoa (for herb-grilled salmon and salad)
Farfalle pasta (for pesto dish)
Orzo (for grilled vegetable dish)
Whole grain crackers (for tapenade)
Pita chips (for guacamole)

Herbs, Spices & Pantry Staples:

Basil, rosemary (for salads and focaccia)
Pine nuts (for pesto)
Olives, capers (for puttanesca and cacciatore)
Olive oil, balsamic vinegar (for dressing and cooking)
Sundried tomatoes (for quiche)
Chimichurri sauce (for steak)

Miscellaneous:

Peanut butter, jelly (for energy bites)
Dark chocolate (for macaroons)
Tapenade (for serving with crackers)

Grocery Shopping List for 50-56 Day Meal Plan

Proteins:

Turkey (for breakfast meatballs)
Squid (for stuffing)

Cottage cheese (for peachy delight)
Gyro meat (for gyros)
Salmon (for bagel and herb-grilled salmon)
Pork tenderloin (for pork with fig and balsamic)
Tuna (for breakfast salad and steak)
Chicken sausage (for skillet)

Dairy and Dairy Alternatives:

Feta cheese (for avocado toast and chickpea salad)
Cream cheese (for bagel)
Greek yogurt (for mousse and parfait)

Fruits and Vegetables:

Spinach (for meatballs and tortellini)
Asparagus (for risotto and grilled side)
Peaches (for cottage cheese delight)
Pomegranate (for mousse)
Avocados (for toast)
Lemons (for zest and dressing)
Tomatoes (for sauce and salsa)
Mixed berries (for parfait)
Portobello mushrooms (for grilling)
Broccoli (for salad)

Grains, Nuts, & Bakery:

Couscous (for tabbouleh and stuffing)
Bagels (for smoked salmon bagel)
Tortellini (preferably with spinach filling)
Penne pasta (for pesto penne)
Almonds (for energy balls and penne)

Dates (for energy balls)

Herbs, Spices & Pantry Staples:

Various fresh herbs (for tabbouleh, meatballs, and chickpea salad)

Balsamic vinegar, figs (for pork tenderloin)
Olive oil (for cooking and dressings)
Lavender (for shortbread)

Miscellaneous:

Honey (for energy balls and cheesecake)
Raspberry (for galettes)
Quinoa (for salad and salmon dish)
White wine (for mussels sauce)

Made in the USA
Las Vegas, NV
02 May 2024

89413551R00057